Attainable
PERFECTION

Three Rarely Used Scriptural Keys

That Simplify Christian Maturity

MICHAEL W. H. HOLCOMB

Attainable Perfection *by* Michael W. H. Holcomb
Copyright © 2009 by Michael W. H. Holcomb
All Rights Reserved.
ISBN: 1-59755-200-3
ISBN13: 978-1-59755-200-4

Published by: ADVANTAGE BOOKS™
www.advbookstore.com

All quotes from the Bible are taken from the King James Version.

The author uses an *upper style* for religious writing, capitalizing the eternal places, nouns and pronouns that refer to God, the word *Church* (when it denotes the world-wide body of believers), and other biblical terminology.

Library of Congress Control Number: 2009938834

Cover Design by Pat Theriault

First Printing: October 2009
09 10 11 12 13 14 15   10 9 8 7 6 5 4 3 2 1
Printed in the United States of America

To my brothers and fellow tag-team preachers in the Strange Fire Seminar, Mark and Matthew.

I love you both!

Bro.-John,
Great to see
you again! Please
keep me in prayer.
Love,
MWHH.

Special thanks to the sisters at The Door Fellowship who helped with the initial editing:

Amy Lekites, Lori McCarty, Kathy McKernan, and Jacque Myers

Table of Contents

THE GARDEN KEY

ONE

Are Christians Supposed to be Perfect?

L et me shock you by stating that those who say "Christians can't be perfect" are being hypocritical; for in every other area of life, they (with everyone else) strive for perfection.

Just look at all those catchy, quotable motivational quips you have undoubtedly encountered. They are everywhere: dentists' lobbies, school stairwells, business offices, country club hallways, locker rooms, airport lounges, gyms, civic centers, youth hangouts, and even church foyers. They are on posters, mugs, buttons, bumper stickers, and the internet. You hear them from teachers and presidents, coaches and CEOs, salesmen, and, yes, pastors. I am talking about all those celebrated words of wisdom that clearly prove mankind's pursuit of perfection. Here are a few of the hundreds out there:

> Those who say it can't be done are usually interrupted by others doing it.
>
> — *Anonymous*

A man can be as great as he wants to be.

— *Vince Lombardi*

The harder the course, the more rewarding the triumph.

— *Anonymous*

If you can dream it, you can do it.

— *Walt Disney*

See what I mean? We all know what it takes to be a winner in business, sports, education, entertainment, and other ambitions that benefit or interest us. For that success we are more than willing to pay the price of sacrifice, discipline, and high standards; yet when it comes to serving the Lord, our flesh prefers to eek out a much lesser offering.

"Nobody expects you to be perfect," "God's grace means you don't have to be perfect," or "You can be perfect in your heart, but you will never be perfect in your behavior" are maxims that, repeated over and over again, are hypnotic, brainwashing devices the devil is using against the Body of Christ. Innocent but ignorant believers are transmitting such doctrinal plague. One effect of such thoughtless parroting has been the development of virtual idolatry in the Church. People set personal pursuit on the throne of their heart because, while they are told God does not demand excellence from them ("Christians aren't perfect, just forgiven."), they are also told the Church really exists to help them reach their ambitions and their dreams. Hence, the idolatry, the reason scads of church members are far more devoted to things like losing their love handles or becoming a pop star than seeking the Kingdom.

No one can serve two masters. The selfish person (religious or not) is inclined to disobey God and fight His authority. Though it is meant to make one feel good, the "Christian's can't be perfect" philosophy only prepares people for the damnation that always follows idolatry and self-worship, for it is written, "Thou shalt not have any other gods before me."[1]

What People Really Hear

Consider the biblical definition of the word *perfect*. As you may guess, it means "complete" and "entire," but beyond that it means "integrity," "prosperity," "repair," "to ripen fruit," and "to satisfy." It also means "the point aimed at," "the conclusion of an act or state," and "the result."[2] Therefore, when churchgoers get behind the pulpit or speak up at a Bible study and reaffirm "nobody's perfect," the message that subconsciously gets imparted is:

* You can never really be mature as a Christian.

* You can never be fully repaired as a person.

* You can never prosper in integrity.

* You will never obtain appropriate results or reach the goal of becoming an overcomer, even though you are a child of God.

Does this sound like good news to you? Does this resemble the potential of God's restoration power?

How about when people repeat the spinoff of the nobody's-perfect doctrine. You know, the one that goes something like "Everybody sins and even Christians are going to continue to sin." Given the nature of iniquity, what are the listeners of this conclusion actually hearing?

* You can count on trespassing against God's righteousness all the time.

* You can expect on a regular basis to do the exact opposite of what the Lord has commanded or to totally ignore what He has commanded.

* You may as well just give into the fact that everyday you are going to do things that God absolutely hates.

It makes no difference what gracious and celebrated theological theories promise. When you remove the wrapping of the nobody's-perfect doctrine, you find nothing but foolish and rotten excuses for living in the filth of ignorance and defeat.

Where There is No Vision

We live in a period in which general society is clamoring for a license to do whatever it wants, however it wants, and whenever it wants, all without blame or consequence. No wonder the saying "you can't be perfect" has become scandalously contagious. Too few are willing to cooperate with any prescribed social standard, let alone a godly one.

Centuries ago, King Solomon, who arguably is the wisest man the world has ever seen, foresaw what would happen if a culture (let alone an individual) threw off wholesome conduct and gave itself over to moral compromise and secular dumbing down:

Where *there is* no vision, the people perish.
— *Proverbs 29:18*

Look how other versions of the Bible interpret that same warning:

Where there is no vision, the people decay.
— *Geneva Bible*[3]

Without a vision is a people naked.
— *Young's Literal Translation*[4]

If people can't see what God is doing, they stumble all over themselves.
— *The Message*[5]

Where there is no message from God, the people don't control themselves.
— *New International Reader's Version*[6]

When people do not accept divine guidance, they run wild.
— *The New Living Translation*[7]

Without guidance from God law and order disappear.
— *Contemporary English Version*[8]

In our Western culture, we have had several decades of living under a *non-* or *anti-*perfection philosophy. Today, the outcome of this social experiment is obvious: a break-the-rules, do-what-feels-good society does not work.

In practically every American town one commonly finds broken families, unruly young people, and scores of fornicators who brazenly parade their perversion in protest of a Christian heritage. There is more corruption than ever before, entertainment with its filth and violence has spun out of control, common sense and good taste are becoming socially extinct, crime is reaching epidemic proportions, and neighborhoods are not the family-friendly places they used to be. All this is the horrible evidence and aftermath of a people living for themselves and behaving according to their own erratic standards of right and wrong, a people who scorn moral—no, *godly*—perfection.

Solomon was right. Without a vision of a righteous God and what He expects from mankind, civilization rots and can look forward to nothing but chaos and ruin.

"Nakedness" and "decay" can also be seen in the modern Church, just as Solomon predicted. Members are "running wild," and "law and order have disappeared" from the lives of many leaders allowing the world to point its fingers and taunt and criticize us with "Weakness. Inconsistency. Mediocrity." Yet, with a standard of nobody's perfect, why should Christians be shocked? Many go around preaching, "We will all sin," but then turn around and mourn, "There is so much garbage in the Church." What are people expecting? They have lost, or in some cases thrown away, their vision of Christ, His righteousness, and the divine call to perfection. Human beings thrive on goals, and when we are not going after God's objectives, we automatically default to those of selfish design. We can sing all the songs we want about hungering for God, we can cry all night long for revival, but in the end *we get what we preach.* And we are preaching self-destruction!

14

What Does the Bible Say?

I am here to give you good news: You *can* operate with satisfactory results in the things of Jesus Christ. You *can* mature into a mighty man or woman who is "fully repaired," fruitful, and influential. You *can* be perfect!

From Old Testament to New, there is a definite target of perfection; and Christians should be encouraged that through Christ, they can and must meet this standard.

"Well," someone will say, "that's not what my preacher preaches. That's not what my denomination believes." Christianity is not about what your preacher, my preacher, or any other earthly authority thinks or believes. This is all about the Ultimate Authority—God and His Word. What does the Lord have to say about perfection?

Be ye therefore perfect, even as your Father which is in heaven is perfect.
                                                — *Matthew 5:48*

But let patience have *her* perfect work, that ye may be perfect and entire, wanting nothing.
                                                — *James 1:4*

Let us cleanse ourselves from all filthiness of the flesh and spirit, perfecting holiness in the fear of God.
                                                — *2 Corinthians 7:1*

15

Let us go on unto <u>perfection</u>,

— Hebrews 6:1

We believers are *commanded* to be upright, circumspect, without sin, and "filled with all the fullness of God."[9] We read in Scripture of people who are specifically described as being perfect or blameless;[10] and just for these upright ones, we find Psalms and Proverbs abundant with promises. First-century Christian workers—those under grace—"labored" to see the Body come to perfection,[11] and both Paul and Peter urged the budding churches to expect completeness and maturity.[12]

Having therefore these promises, dearly beloved, let us cleanse ourselves from all filthiness of the flesh and spirit, perfecting holiness in the fear of God.

— 2 Corinthians 7:1

Let every one that nameth the name of Christ depart from iniquity.

— 2 Timothy 2:19b

"Wherefore, beloved, seeing that ye look for such things, be diligent that ye may be found of him in peace, without spot, and blameless.

— 2 Peter 3:14

Sure, you have tons of concerns by now. Later on, I deal with the subjects of human inferiority, making mistakes, and what God's idea of perfection is and is not (biblical truths which I believe will revolutionize your life). But first, you need to have right goals, or rather, right faith anchored in your soul. This generation embraces a philosophy of disobedience and destruction, a message that rebels against the clear will of the Lord. You, however, can avoid such poisonous lies and the consequences that follow.

God is not cruel. Remember that! He has never commanded you to be or do something beyond your ability. If He has commanded perfection from you, it is because He, through Jesus Christ, has given you everything you need to grow strong and complete in Him. You need to know that His perfection is attainable.

The Mission of Jesus

The greatest need of the Church today is to get a full revelation of the Lord Jesus Christ and His ongoing work in the world. Repentance and conversion are just the start of what God has purposed through Jesus. All believers are familiar with the sacrifice of the cross and the mercies of the blood; but too few perceive the significance of the empty tomb: There is power for a new life.

Jesus Christ came to save—YES!—but the Bible says He came to save in order that He might bring "many sons unto glory."[13] Glory is more than Heaven; glory includes perfection, right here, right now. The whole reason Christ sends apostles, prophets, evangelists, pastors, and teachers to His Body is for "the perfecting of the saints."[14] Jesus is passionately working to make your life perfect in all the ways of God.[15]

The Bible says:

Christ also loved the church, and gave himself for it; that he might sanctify and cleanse it with the washing of water by the word, that he might present it to himself a glorious church, not having spot, or wrinkle, or any such thing; but that it should be holy and without blemish.

- Ephesians 5:25-27

Now the God of peace … make you perfect in every good work to do his will, working in you that which is wellpleasing in his sight, through Jesus Christ; to whom *be* glory for ever and ever. Amen.

— Hebrews 13:20-21

For it is God which worketh in you both to will and to do of *his* good pleasure.

— Philippians 2:13

Jesus came to fill the cracks in humanity, to add the missing pieces, and to restore what was broken down. As a man, He is our crowning glory, epitomizing everything expected of we who are created in God's image. He is the One, True Light who identifies with every soul on earth[16] and who reveals life's reality. Jesus Christ is the Author and Finisher, the Beginner and Perfecter[17] of our humanity as well as our faith.[18] If He preached perfection, it was because He came for that purpose.

When someone hears, "*You* can't be perfect," they soon begin saying, "*I* can't be perfect," and the full revelation of Jesus and the expectation He instills in them is stolen from their hearts. They lose the Christian race even before they have begun. Why not, instead, train each other with the motivational sayings of the Bible? You know, the ones we quote when we are seeking God to give us something we want. Hey, sinners use worldly wisdom for worldly perfection, how much better when saints use godly wisdom for godly perfection.

> If God *be* for us, who *can be* against us?
> — *Romans 8:31*

> I can do all things through Christ which strengtheneth me.
> — *Philippians 4:13*

> ...Greater is he that is in you, than he that is in the world.
> — *1 John 4:4*

> But my God shall supply all your need according to his riches in glory by Christ Jesus.
> — *Philippians 4:19*

After knowing these promises, I am sure there are those of you who still will be stressed out by the mere thought of being complete, mature, and blameless. Well, I guarantee the pressure you feel is not from God. Christ has made living for Him well within our reach. His willingness to help is as profound and impressive as one would see in any good, earthly father. That helpless sense you have has to do with something else, something imperfect going on in the background of your mind, something keeping you from the liberty of Christ's perfection.

CHAPTER ONE REVIEW

1. We all know how to give 100% to selfish pursuits; yet when it comes to serving the Lord, our flesh prefers a different standard.

2. Without the vision of a righteous God or a goal of righteous living, there is personal and cultural chaos and destruction.

3. The Bible makes it clear that Christians can and must be perfect.

4. God never commands you to be or do something beyond your ability. In Christ, He gives you everything you need.

5. Jesus is passionately working to perfect you and all other believers.

TWO

Forbidden Perfection

A gain, God is not cruel and oppressive. In calling you to perfection, He does not ask you to do things you are incapable of achieving neither is He sentencing you to some fanatical lifestyle where the slightest mistake brings fierce punishment. Relax and trust in the Lord! There is absolutely no reason to be overwhelmed. Jesus said:

> My yoke *is* easy, and my burden is light.
> — *Matthew 11:30*

Sure, there are Christian deeds you are to develop, but none requiring elite skills or rare talents. Yes, there are disciplines of faith that you need to exercise, but none so bizarre that they conflict with everything ordinary and everyday. The Lord was saying here that a lifestyle dedicated to following Him—one that takes up His yoke and His burden—is doable, especially because Jesus promised to help us!

The problem—and the panic—comes in when we approach God's perfection with carnal prejudices and misunderstandings, that is, *our* concepts of perfection.

Because of the fall, humans have inherent, wrong ideas of what perfection is supposed to look like. In practically every religion of the world, some sort of standard has been created for perfection, but each is an inaccessible cloud. Even without religious models, our *terra firma* expectations for personal excellence are clumsy, unfair weights. To us, being a perfect person means:

- Having an ideal past (or at least having no links with a bad one).
- Having no quirks, weaknesses, or blind spots.
- Being incapable of making a mistake, getting in trouble, or falling into error.
- Being beyond criticism, embarrassment, or frustration.
- Never being vulnerable.
- Never having setbacks or regrets.
- Having the best of all character traits.
- Possessing unbreakable, unbeatable will power.
- Always having a great day.
- Always feeling good about yourself.
- Always being right.

These are but a few of our extreme, subconscious goals. What they really reflect, however, is an unrealistic notion that we can evolve into someone who needs nothing or nobody. We desperately search for that magic pill, that autopilot mode that supposedly will guarantee us a permanent, self-reliant status. Our brand of perfection is what I call *forbidden perfection* and it reeks of ripened pride. Fool's gold is what it is; and what a bitter disappointment for those of us who have discovered such!

Perfection Is Not a Ladder

What one model best describes forbidden perfection? The one most intimidating is a ladder. Most of us picture life as a series of continuous steps, levels to which one must progressively rise by means of immense effort and after a good deal of time. Well, there are serious flaws with this ladder concept.

To put it simply, life on a ladder is harsh and cruel. Those who are seen as being above are envied if not considered threatening while those who are below are looked at as being helplessly inferior. If that's not enough, those possessed with going to the top fail to see in this kill-or-be-killed climb that *there is no top!* No matter how high you go, there is always another rung above you. Not even supposed champions of the model realize the ladder awards no satisfying trophies.

The most serious flaw, however, is the perception of failure. Life on the loftier rungs may be impressive, but mistakes up there are unforgiving. Many who have crashed at the bottom never try again. The struggle and the sacrifice to regain their former position are (in their minds) hopelessly unaffordable. Most people see their life as being at the bottom, looking up to an impossible ascent.

As a pastor, I have talked with person after person who came to the conclusion they could never make it with God because, to them, their slip-up meant losing all spiritual progress. They still loved the Lord, but while they viewed other church members as moving forward, they saw themselves as only going backward. Praise the Lord, I have been able to open the Bible and give them God's pattern of perfection!

Unlike heathenism and cults, which employ the ladder model, God's blueprints for human development do not include ascending ranks or planes. Instead, we find the Great Creator treats our existence much more down-to-earth.

God sees our lives as being a garden having seasons, harvests, and with plants in various stages of growth.

Later on, I am going to show you just how significant this divine model is, but what I want this to mean right now is that *God's perfection is realistic and within reach.* We will never receive divine assistance if we work life on a ladder. Why? Because God does not build ladders, He grows gardens.

Sanctimonious Perfection

Let me present another form of forbidden perfection. Throughout history, church bodies have formed their own ladder models. To this day, scores of believers, loaded with unnecessary burdens, are undergoing grueling climbs, all because a few leaders impose upon their consciences standards that are overly particular and severely out of proportion.

This type of forbidden perfection is what I call *sanctimonious perfection,* and it is more concerned with an exterior appearance of right than with an interior substance of right. Sanctimonious perfection always adds to the Gospel and, therefore, bogs down simplicity.

First, there are the rules of sanctimonious perfection. I'm not talking about the life-giving commandments of Christ. I'm

24

talking about picky, inconsistent rulings on costume, diet, transportation, matrimonial intimacy, conduct of a service— extra-biblical church laws that are officially spelled out and then fortified with Heaven-or-Hell consequences.

Let me give you an example. Suppose that in my church, many of the good, solid saints have been in the habit of drinking strawberry-flavored milk. Somewhere along the line we notice that new people coming in, who do not drink strawberry-flavored milk, are rude, vulgar, and annoyingly immature in the things of God. We want the new people to behave like the established people (that's a good thing), but we equate strawberry-flavored milk with spiritual maturity (that's a bad thing). Now let's suppose that we not only make it a church membership requirement to drink strawberry-flavored milk, but worse, we begin preaching that without strawberry in their milk, God's wrath is upon the non-flavor crowd (after all, they are rude, vulgar, and immature). What have we just done? We have taken the focus away from root issues, which the Bible addresses, and put it on artificial righteousness. We have destroyed a pristine environment of divine principles and replaced it with one of toxic snobbery and cannibal-like criticism: "I've got strawberry in my milk, you don't," and "Your milk doesn't have *enough* strawberry."

Of course this scenario is far-fetched, but so are all the other non-moral, irrelevant, uninspired standards that people pass off as being true Christian essentials. It does not matter if its policies are initially designed to fix problems, sanctimonious perfection will *always* hold its people in fear, bondage, and a pathetic infancy, so that even the eager and the involved are doomed to spiritual decay.

Second, and if the rules were not enough, it is my observation that those given to sanctimonious perfection always have such severe ideas and ideals about spiritual things. You rarely find one among them that truly shows satisfaction in their walk. Like the proverbial hamster running on a go-nowhere, stationary wheel, they are forever restless in exercising religious superstitions. To the sanctimonious, being perfect means reaching a stage where one:

- Is never tempted.
- Never makes an oversight in his walk.
- Always has *feelings* of brotherly love, divine grace, supernatural movement, and the like.
- Is automatically motivated to perform godly duties such as prayer, witnessing, and going to church.
- Is so heavenly minded, he can go without modern creature comforts and get by with only the most basic, bare essentials.
- Is so spiritually minded, he can successfully abstain from sensations like excitement, recreation, or even passion.
- Has finally overcome all personal quirks and self-perceived obstacles (internal and external).
- Has gone beyond pain, lack, weakness, and commonality to attain uninterrupted tranquility of the soul.

What Sanctimony Produces

For a number of people, sanctimonious perfection has an incredibly strong pull. Some like the idea of religious elitism or the mysteries and complexities of their church's formality. Some have a relative, a tradition, or a similar kind of soul tie that personally obligates them. Still others are attracted because they have a guilt-based notion they can cleanse themselves through intense religious formulas. Regardless of their reasons, those who are addicted would rather waste their lives chasing sanctimony's elusive rainbows than admit its uselessness.

For the majority, however, sanctimonious perfection forces them into a frustrated explosion of absolute rebellion. Oh, yes! The high-and-mighty attitude of counterfeit religion drives people from the very Jesus it claims to represent. I have seen it.

Understand the devil is behind *all* our carnal ideas of perfection. His snake oil sales pitch "ye shall be as gods" was what got us into trouble in the first place. The enemy actually *wants* people to practice sanctimonious perfection. Using man's selfish desire to escape to some parallel universe of higher significance, he encourages people to pile on unwarranted and unachievable religiosity. Then when they are wore down and properly discouraged he makes an incredibly crafty flip-flop. "See, you can't be perfect," he says. "You've tried so hard and you can't make it. Give up! Turn from God. He's the one who wants you to be perfect anyway." So multitudes turn from the prospect of being perfect; and while people are walking away from false and self-righteous standards, they also give up on that which is good, godly, and attainable—just as the enemy planned.

Jesus taught that through religious tradition—that is, "forbidden perfection"—man actually neutralizes the otherwise powerful Word of God.[1] If God forbids sanctimonious perfection, if it saps the life out of saints, churches, and entire denominations, it is because such a pursuit is defective, partial, and in no way fruit-bearing maturity.

The point is, to the sanctimonious mind giving one's all to God *should be* something hard and complex. For this reason, those given to sanctimony are more preoccupied with suppressing personality, sentiment, and sense than with developing principle and discernment. To them, holiness is not a virtuous *advantage* that overcomes the world, it is more like a *dare* that proves personal spirituality: "If you *really* loved God you wouldn't mind this custom, that tradition, or going without such and such. If you were *really* devout, you would be able to endure the disciplines of our particular sect."

These days there are those who practice a *non-perfection* sanctimony, who dare believers that if they are really sincere they will have a church culture that is casual, cool, and without rules. This peer-pressured piety is just as anemic and artificial as the traditional kind!

In the end, lovers of sanctimony love the ladder, that forbidden pursuit which promises to make them look oh, so good. Yet the above goals and all other such churchy fantasies are more than distractions, they are corrupting concepts, harmful ambitions, and counterfeit values. No wonder Christian people repeat the false statement "You can't be perfect": in the past, they approached God with unrealistic goals and holier-than-thou ideals, and subsequently they have become discouraged, intimidated, and spiritually exhausted. Even so, frustration from a false standard of perfection is no excuse for rejecting a godly standard. That, too, is forbidden.

Leave the Wrong, Take the Right

It's time for you to wake up and throw the devil off your back. He is the manipulator who is pressuring you, telling you that being an overcomer might be possible for saintly geniuses, but it is too difficult for an average believer like you. Do not be duped by his twisted logic and do not let him use your bad experience with false perfection to prevent you from the real thing.

God gives us a goal of an ordinary, everyday perfection for an ordinary, everyday world. Your answer is "looking unto Jesus," for He gives you something better than fantasy faith and plastic do's and don'ts. He gives you the guidance, the strength, and the authority to triumph in the realities of life. It does not matter how you see your performance or how you feel about yourself, you must continue relying on Jesus. He is your one tangible guarantee of attaining perfection.

Achieving in the Kingdom is simpler than you think. But are you willing to swallow your pride and accept that simplicity? Will you get off the crowded highway that leads to a futile, corrupt perfection and submit to the doable kind Christ offers?

I cannot speak for you, but I know that I want the freedom that is in the unpretentious, unsophisticated perfection of Jesus. I want real maturity. I want real spirituality. I want something that can never be found by those on a ladder.

CHAPTER TWO REVIEW

1. God's perfection is doable, but man's idea of perfection is not.

2. Perfection is not a ladder with never ending levels. Instead, God's pattern for our lives resembles a garden, a place where there is room and time for growth.

3. One form of forbidden perfection is what I call "sanctimonious perfection," man's religious ideals that add to God's ways, making them incredibly complex and difficult.

4. Sanctimonious perfection damages the Church just as much as sin; for it keeps people in fear, bondage, and spiritual infancy.

5. Sanctimonious perfection actually neutralizes the otherwise powerful Word of God, producing in your life no maturity at all.

THREE

God's Perfection

I shall never forget August 7, 2007. That was the day God gave me this message. I wrote 180 pages of notes in three days. It was all I could do to keep up with the leading of the Spirit.

One of the first things the Lord showed me was that perfection is like a garden because we are like a garden. Being of the earth, our existence resembles and flows with the rest of creation. We begin as a seed, we grow to a species' prime, and we produce after our kind. We go through seasons in our lives (we actually use that terminology) and we have personal times that can be compared with planting and replanting, uprooting and pruning, grafting and watering—just like a garden.

The Lord also showed me that, in fact, *He* views our life as a garden. Look at the language of the Bible. Being redeemed, God calls us "a planting of the Lord"[1] who must be "rooted in" the Lord Jesus Christ.[2] We are reminded that "whatsoever a man soweth, that shall he also reap."[3] Believers are encouraged to bear fruit[4] and warned what happens if we stop bearing.[5] Even in speaking about the end of the world, God uses agrarian expressions:

Thrust in thy sickle, and reap: for the time is come
for thee to reap; for the harvest of the earth is ripe.
— *Revelation 14:15*

Life is a garden, not a ladder. Understand how a garden works, and you will understand how you work and how perfection works. But before I go any further, there is one point I need to emphasize:

Perfection is not a man thing, it' s a God thing.

When the Almighty appeared to the 99-year-old Abraham, the Lord did not simply say, "Be perfect." No, He said, "Walk before me, and be thou perfect."[6] Perfection is about walking before God. In walking before man, we can appear and act much differently than who we really are, but pretended agreement and mere imitation make no impression on God. The Lord looks for a spirit of conformity. He knows if the inward is pure, whole, and focused, the outward will follow.

The Bible shows us that at the Last Day, every person will stand before God and give an individual accounting to Him. God will not judge us according to popular opinions, world religions, or by our explanations of how we behaved. We will face our Maker and He alone will measure and assess our lives by His pre-established principles. The only thing that will matter then—the only thing that matters now—will be our complete, total, and full commitment to Jesus Christ—His covenant, His Anointing, His leadership, and His commandments.

Perfection. It's a God thing done God's way.

Perfection's Produce

Now if life is a garden, what is a complete, mature, perfect person supposed to grow? If not ladder levels, what does God want from you? What are you to work toward?

Do you remember the parable Jesus told about the sower who "went out to sow his seed?" What was the seed? Jesus revealed it plainly, "The seed is the word of God."[7] So, if it was the Word which was being planted, what was to be the expected harvest? You guessed it, the Word.

Let me tell you something about that Old Black Book. It is not just paper and ink, chapter and verse, and it is certainly not a menu of pick-and-choose items. It is a seed sack, filled with divine kernels, eager to produce in you what is ever of God. Some today are foolishly saying that Christianity needs to be "upgraded," "reinvented" to fit our times, as if the calendar or popular opinion has changed truth. However, man lives by the commandments and declarations that God has *already* spoken. The Word is healing, health, strength, stability, authority, and might. It brings law and order, guarantees peace and prosperity, and it gives you and me a future and a hope. Understand above all else the Word is the revelation of a *Someone*, not just a something. That Bible of yours is all about Jesus.

In the beginning was the Word, and the Word was with God, and the Word was God. ... And the Word was made flesh, and dwelt among us, (and we beheld his glory, the glory as of the only begotten of the Father,) full of grace and truth.

— *John 1:1, 14*

Jesus of Nazareth embodies the will of God for humanity. Being sent from Heaven, He accomplished all righteousness, fulfilled all Scripture, and faithfully told us of the Father. This and much more make Him *The* Word of God, and in being the Word, Jesus has the Word.

Jesus Christ came with a greater, more important message than any other prophet before or after Him. He made it very clear that His teaching and preaching has supreme significance. He declared:

- You are a wise man building your house on a rock **if** you hear and keep His sayings.[8]
- You will know Him and thus know the truth **if** you obey His commandments.[9]
- You are His friend **if** you do what He tells you.[10]
- You can enter the Kingdom of Heaven **if** you do the will of God as spoken by Him.[11]

In revealing Christ, God has given mankind the seed of His Word and now He expects us to accept and grow that Seed. Furthermore, Jesus Himself is the Word we are to produce. The Bible says that if we abide in Him, we will bring forth fruit[12] acceptable to God. Conforming to the image of God's dear Son is the simple goal of perfection.

Cooperation

Allow me to show you something else. There are several passages in the Bible that sum up God's will and Word to humanity. For instance, Solomon said:

Fear the Lord and keep his commandments.[13]

Micah said:
> Do justly ... love mercy ...walk humbly with thy
> God.[14]

Peter said:
> Add to your faith virtue; and to virtue knowledge;
> and to knowledge temperance; and to temperance
> patience; and to patience godliness; and to godliness
> brotherly kindness; and to brotherly kindness
> charity.[15]

Jesus had the best summarization:
> Thou shalt love the Lord thy God with all thy heart,
> and with all thy soul, and with all thy mind ...[and]
> thou shalt love thy neighbour as thyself.[16]

Did you see anything in these lists that are above and beyond physical power? Is there anything excessive, mystical, or severe here? No, and what is wonderful about the Lord is His standard of perfection is not locked behind cultural and privileged contexts nor is it hidden by deep secrets and lucky shortcuts like the religions of men. God has put His Word in clear terms, universally observed by and familiar to the human experience; simple enough that the most crude and primitive among us can relate.

Jesus fits.

The real question of perfection is not "Can I do it?" Rather, it is "Will I receive and cooperate with what God is planting in the earth—Jesus Christ?"

When Christ returns, He will be looking specifically for individuals who have perfect faith in Him.[17] A person with faith has more than head knowledge and does more than verbally confess bible doctrine. (Even devils believe and quote Scripture.[18]) He has a substance that is evident to all. He who has real faith rejects every other way of thinking and every personal expectation of how life should be. He does not practice forbidden perfection but is sold out to an unconditional trust in the Christ of the Word and the Word of Christ.

Remember, it's all about the Seed.

Multiple Harvests

Now that you know what you are to produce, you should know a few things about how you are to produce.

A few months before getting *Attainable Perfection* published, a friend of mine inquired about its progress. Naturally, I gave him a rundown of what I had just been writing. With a little smile and a whole lot of sincerity, he asked, "So, once you have attained perfection, where do you go from there?" The following is the answer the Lord gave me.

The ladder model falsely gives us the impression that levels or aspects of life can be achieved, mastered, and then possessed once and for all, like the way a student passes a school grade. Take forgiveness for example. We think we can learn about forgiveness, build up to forgiveness, exemplify forgiveness, and—voila!—we have conquered the forgiveness grade. From now on, forgiveness will come automatically. This, to our carnal mind, is perfection; but reality is very different.

There is no such thing as mastering life to the point that it becomes effortless and your results, predictable; and in the

Kingdom, there is no such thing as one-time harvests. "Been there, done that" is a saying we cannot apply to future behavior. Understand, oh planting of the Lord, that reaping is a repeated occurrence. Throughout your life, there will be many times you will have to produce the same goods as you did before. In other words, perfection is not a class position; it is an ongoing practice of producing the things of Jesus.

Just because you forgave someone ten years ago, does not mean that nowadays you are Captain Forgiveness, desensitized to bullets of anger or punches of tempted revenge. What pride! Next time around, you may actually encounter a worse situation with worse feelings. You must, nevertheless, yield the fruit of forgiveness all over again. You will have to plant the seeds *again*, water the crops *again*, and get out the harvesting equipment *again*. All of this means regular interaction with a living Savior, Jesus the Word.

The real advantage of having already gone through something is that now you can foresee some do's and don'ts, you know the Word of the Lord better, and you have experiential hope of what the Lord can do. Other than that, it still requires sweat and time in your garden. Once the harvest is over, however, God looks *again* and He sees something besides what your will or selfishness did. He sees Jesus and His reaction. He sees the Word. You have sown Christ and now Christ has been formed—and Father says *again*, "Just what I wanted! That's perfect!"

This is growing in grace, and this is exactly why a truly perfect person will never be heard saying, "Look at me. I'm perfect." Should they claim sight, they would become blind. Should they claim riches, they would become poor; the credit belongs to God and His Word. Besides, they are too busy to stop for such self-elevating, ladder nonsense. They are working in the fields with Jesus, looking forward to multiple harvests in this life and one great harvest in the life to come.

> Not as though I had already attained, either were already perfect: but I follow after, if that I may apprehend that for which also I am apprehended of Christ Jesus. Brethren, I count not myself to have apprehended: but *this* one thing *I do,* forgetting those things which are behind, and reaching forth unto those things which are before, I press toward the mark for the prize of the high calling of God in Christ Jesus. Let us therefore, as many as be perfect, be thus minded ...
>
> — *Philippians 3:12-15*

Garden Chores

There is a house near mine whose gardens, I am told, were once picturesque and lush. Children playing amid the blooms and flowering shrubs, imagined themselves in fairy-tale lands. It was a lovely place. The owner spent many long and happy hours amongst her living things, and even found time to invest her credible skills and knowledge in the local garden club, a telling testimony of the gardens indeed.

But that was a long time ago.

Today, there is but an occasional blush of color in that lonely piece of property. The plants that have managed to survive are either hidden or grossly overgrown. Nobody stops to "wow" any longer. Nobody comes in search of make-believe. The garden just sits there, quietly waiting for the day when a working hand will restore its past glory.

Here is a painful fact: *it is possible to go from prosperity to ruin, from perfection to imperfection.*

People may think this is unfair, but when it comes to getting ahead in life, fairness is a synthetic hope of ladder thinking. Only those who believe they have been successful in climbing rungs expect their position to take priority over their practice. In the reality of the garden, however:

> Whatsoever a man soweth, that shall he also reap.
> — *Galatians 6:7b*

You cannot continue reaping perfection if you do not continue sowing perfection.

Many church people assume that when an individual falls from Christian behavior, it is because he always had a particular fault, a flaw that was never corrected. This conclusion, like the idea of fairness, is simply not true. Samson of the Bible serves as an ideal example.[19] He was called of God before he was ever conceived. You do not get a more pure start than that. Samson was raised with a strict set of standards that guaranteed his gift and leadership. At a young age, he was moved on by the Holy Spirit to become God's judge to God's people. Samson was perfect. Yet you know the story. Something happened to his perfection. Something perverted it, weakened it, and eventually, something ended it.

To keep on producing perfect harvests, you must keep up with the upkeep. *The length of time you have been a Christian is irrelevant*; you will regularly have to face and conquer temptation, laziness, selfishness, discouragement, and even exhaustion. You will regularly have to build up your spirit by prayer, praise, reading the Word, Christian fellowship, and the like. Ignore these basic chores simply because you are bored with the work and your soul will wither and be ravaged by the enemy. Like Samson, you will cease from being productive.

Oh, how many Samsons have we seen in the Church? How many mighty heroes of the faith have fought their way to incredible victories and world-shaking influence only to end up shaved of their anointing, grinding away in some blind, dumb rut? No doubt, these former champions left the simplicity of the garden model, built a ladder in their heart, and concluded that they had reached a height of immunity and invulnerability. Their sad loss should teach us to keep a healthy garden.

> And let us not be weary in well doing: for in due season we shall reap, if we faint not.
> — *Galatians 6:9*

Having said that, I am happy to inform you that if you have neglected your garden, if you are a backslidden Samson *you have hope*. As long as you have life in you and can call on the name of Jesus, *you have hope*. Things can be cleaned up, refurbished, fixed, and put to use again. By God's marvelous grace, you can still defeat the enemy; you can still have another harvest.

Garden perfection, real perfection is about working with Christ Jesus. Keep up with the upkeep of that relationship and you are safe. Say, "Lord, I am dependant upon you," and you mature and stay mature.

Jesus will indeed push you beyond your own standards and satisfaction. Guaranteed! He will stretch you because He knows you can handle much more than you think. Yet, He has promised to work right next to you in your garden.

> Lo, I am with you alway, *even* unto the end of the world.
>
> — *Matthew 28:20*

Now Time

Another principle that will really encourage you in the faith is one of the happiest differences between the garden and the ladder models, and it has to do with time.

When you are on a ladder, it is quantity of levels, not quality of the climb that is most important. How much is behind and how much is ahead are the measures of your development, but now there is a problem. Focusing on what you *have* accomplished and what you *have yet* to accomplish only breed frustration. Your fulfillment, inspiration, and significance will always be far off in past and future horizons; while that which is right in front of you will always be regarded as temporary and therefore substandard.

Jesus, on the other hand, taught:

> Take therefore no thought for the morrow: for the morrow shall take thought for the things of itself. Sufficient unto the day *is* the evil thereof.
>
> — *Matthew 6:34*

What wisdom! What truth from the lips of the Master!

You can never exist in yesterday; you can never be in tomorrow. There is really only one day in which you live and it is called *today*. There is really only one experience you can control and it is called *now*. But guess what! You can deal with today; you can take care of now.

God instructs you to live in the present; therefore, *the now* is where your greatest concentration should be. Yes, you should plan for what is ahead and take care of unfinished business from what is behind. Otherwise, sweating about yesterday or tomorrow only messes up today, because life runs in now time.

I know people with such anxiety about backsliding somewhere down the road, they presently refuse to become a Christian. "I don't want to be a hypocrite," they say, but what they are after is totally impossible. They wish to control a time frame other than the one they occupy. You may laugh, but yesterday and tomorrow people develop many such foolish ideas. God calls you to be a today person because it is the now-time mindset that sees the truth.

> As the Holy Ghost saith, To day if ye will hear his voice, harden not your hearts … exhort one another daily, while it is called To day; lest any of you be hardened through the deceitfulness of sin.
> — *Hebrews 3:7-8, 13*

If you want to grow in grace, learn to live in the now. It is like planting corn in your garden. You put the seeds in the ground and two weeks later you look and there are little green sprigs popping out of the dirt. Know what you are going to say? "Perfect! My corn is growing." Though it is tiny and weak, at that moment you will be incredibly happy with your little crop. When you go out several weeks later and find knee-high stalks, know what you are going to say? "Perfect! My corn is growing." Though they have yet to produce anything edible, you will be pleased. When you see the tassels just beginning, you are going to say, "Perfect! My corn is growing." Though the fruit itself is your ultimate harvest, you know the shoot, the stalk, and the tassel are growths that are all essential parts of the plant. You know that each stage must have its now time. That is the way in which God is gracious to us.

Though you may have things yet to achieve and accomplish, as long as you are currently cooperating with all that is presently available, God sees your development as being perfect and He is pleased. This, God's enabling acceptance that moves you forward in His will, is what grace is all about; and it works in now time

Do not get discouraged or bored with the little things of life. Take advantage of their convenience, profit from their importance—and stop worrying so much! If you continue sowing the Seed in your life (thinking the Word, speaking the Word, being around people of the Word), the harvest will come. Realize that growing here, growing there, growing everyday is the divine (and gratifying) process of the garden.

The first time I planted lilies, I was surprised at how deep their bulbs needed to be buried. The ones I was particularly excited about, the white Casablancas, had to be placed 8 inches down, deeper than the rest. After several weeks, the other lilies were above ground and doing well, but I saw nothing of the white ones. I wondered if moles or rot had destroyed them. I decided to investigate; but after digging two or three handfuls of dirt, I found young shoots, strong and healthy, working their way to the top. I was embarrassed at my impatience and put the dirt back, and soon the beautiful Casablancas were boasting of the largest, most fragrant blooms of all the other flowers.

Be patient with God and His time. Perfection is the process as well as the product, so do not get nervous, and forget about looking at the growth stages of others or thinking about all the Kingdom aspects you have yet to practice. Just focus on Jesus, listen and obey His voice, and:

> Rest in the LORD, and wait patiently for him … those that wait upon the LORD, they shall inherit the earth.
> — *Psalms 37:7-9*

It's Only Hard When …

When my dad was a young preacher, one of the brothers in the church came to him complaining of having a lust problem. Yes, he regularly prayed, read his Bible, and came to church; but still, the guy could not shake dirty thoughts and desires. He was discouraged. Come to find out, however, this man was frequently going to a local strip club. No wonder religious exercise failed to be effective! No wonder developing into a mature, overcoming child of God was difficult business. He was trying what never works!

Basically, there are two times when serving God is *not* easy. The first is when we, like the man I just described, attempt to mix selfish and carnal ways with God's will.

Coming to maturity means full surrender and total unity with the Harvester because Jesus refuses to compromise His way of doing things. He will not live with sin. He will not pool resources with forbidden perfection. He will not go along with differing opinions or explore other viewpoints, no matter how much sense they seem to make to you. Yet if Jesus is narrow, it is because He knows He is the only and authentic means to life.

Some say of the Christian life, "It's so *hard*. I've been saved for all these years and I'm still so far from where I should be. When is the Lord going to do something for me?" Stop whining and stop blaming God. If there is struggle in your Christian walk, if your yoke is not easy and your burden is not light, it is because you are fighting Jesus, "kicking against the pricks" as He called it.[20] You have to get rid of all your own carefully selected seeds (yes, even the religious ones) and never reach for them again. *You cannot grow both your will and God's.*

Do you know why worriers get ulcers? Man was not designed for worry. Do you know why many people are depressed? Man was not designed for unforgiveness. Do you know why sinners experience guilt? Man was not designed to follow selfish desires.

You were designed to grow and mature into the image of Jesus Christ, and nothing else will balance your life but Him and His Word. Jesus is how you are to live. He is humanity's true pattern, God's attainable perfection.

The other time when serving the Lord is hard is when you do it with a poor attitude. It is of no consequence if you are very correct and very careful in your religiosity, God hates half-heartedness and He blesses no offering that lacks the seasoning of joy.

Because thou servedst not the LORD thy God with joyfulness, and with gladness of heart, for the abundance of all *things*; Therefore shalt thou serve thine enemies which the LORD shall send against thee ...

— *Deuteronomy 28:47-48b*

God's commandments "are not grievous,"[21] they are a "delight,"[22] and we are commanded as saints to "rejoice in the Lord."[23] Joy is one of the biggest secrets to serving Christ and being an overcomer in the Kingdom. What many people call reverence and holiness is nothing more than stinking sanctimony, void of joy and coming from the devil. Yes, the devil! Satan does not want you *enjoying* the things of God; and if he cannot get you away from the Lord, then like a science specimen in formaldehyde, he will try locking you up with sanctimony, convincing you to keep your faith quiet, private, formal, and solemn. To become strong in the faith, however, you must get into serving Jesus. Only when "the joy of the Lord is your strength"[24] does God's glory come upon you bringing ease and stimulating maturity (something totally unknown to grumblers and the half-hearted).

But be filled with the Spirit; speaking to yourselves in psalms and hymns and spiritual songs, singing and making melody in your heart to the Lord.

— *Ephesians 5:18b-19*

As a pastor, I have heard people say, "I tried going to church and stuff, but it didn't work for me." Every time I have heard that, I have seen a person who gave the Lord *less* than 100% of his energy, his enthusiasm, or his commitment. Oh, he knew how to give 100% and then some to drugs, sex, and the imaginary good life. He exercised remarkable discipline and sacrifice when pursuing that which is completely selfish. Yet when it came to Jesus and God's life, fullness, and power, all the person could do was complain of being under too much pressure.

I feel the Holy Ghost when I write this: God may be free with His grace, but that does not mean God is cheap. Jesus said the Kingdom of Heaven is like a treasure hid in a field, and the only way to get that treasure is to sell everything you have and buy the field. The only way you are going to find God's love is to sell out to Jesus and make Him the joy of your life. If you could give everything to death, bondage, and corruption before you were saved, you can certainly give everything to life, liberty, and righteousness after you are saved.

God's garden is reality, His Word is life, and His perfection is doable. The good news is, it costs what is completely satisfying and absolutely affordable: your all.

CHAPTER THREE REVIEW

1. Perfection is not a man thing, it is a God thing.

2. The harvest God expects you to grow is the Word which is by Jesus and in Jesus.

3. The real question of perfection is not "Can I do it?" Rather, it is "Will I receive and cooperate with Jesus?"

4. Life is not about one-time harvests. Regardless of how experienced you are in the Lord, you will have to produce the same virtues over and over again.

5. It is possible to go from perfection to imperfection.

6. Garden work means maintenance, and unless you keep up with the upkeep you will cease to be productive.

7. You only live in one time frame: now; but you can deal with now. Remember, God's grace is in the now.

8. Two things are not easy when serving God. First, when we attempt to mix selfish and carnal ways with God's will. Second, when we approach the things of God with a poor attitude.

FOUR

Dealing with Mistakes Perfectly

D o you know what the world needs to see? A Christian who knows what to do when he when he makes a mistake! Yes, dealing with mistakes is part of attaining God's perfection, and it all starts by admitting that we are plain, old creatures of the earth, inferior to the Creator, the forces of the natural world, and even our own aspirations for immortality.

Facing this is not easy. It screams against our self-confidence. Oh yes, we are intensely aware of our own blind spots, vulnerabilities, and inconsistencies; and when we think back at past actions, we even confess to lopsided strengths and dumb, defective characteristics. Yet we still tend to choke on the truth of being less than a super hero. However, though we be lesser and deficient beings, *it is within that sphere of inferiority that we are used of God.* Clay jars we are, yet the Bible says the treasure of God's glory rests in these earthen vessels[1]—but wait! The revelation does not stop there.

> And [the Lord] said unto me, <u>My grace is sufficient for thee</u>: for my strength is made perfect in weakness. Most gladly therefore will I rather glory

in my infirmities, <u>that the power of Christ may rest upon me.</u>

— *2 Corinthians 12:9*

We need to recognize the potential of our own perfection *has never been within us*; it has always been, it will always be in "the power of Christ."

Jesus of Nazareth came as God manifest in the flesh.[2] Sensation, energy, or idea is not the medium of His contact with us. Jesus was revealed in the setting of our very own subordinate humanity; but in so coming, He broke the mortal mold of inevitable failure and paved the way for us to be fully repaired, completely capable of producing suitable results.

Jesus Christ completes us and only when we face our faulty makeup, forget our pride, and build on Him is there any maturity and fulfillment in this life. *Our humanity may be a handicap but it is no mistake*, and though we will never be invincible gods we can, through Christ, be perfect human beings.

Dealing with Our Quirks

Christians need to know how to respond to their individual quirks, those personality mistakes that are not necessarily sins but are, nevertheless, troublesome. Dealing with quirks is actually like dealing with temptation.

A few years ago, a guy began attending our mid-week home meeting. He was newly saved and very eager to serve the Lord, but after several months he came to me and told me that he was seriously struggling in his faith. He said that he was

50

having "bad" weeks. He told me that, yes, he had weeks when he believed he was on top of things and doing great; but mostly he said he was failing to measure up to the Christian lifestyle. I asked him point blank about certain sins. No, he was not doing this and, no, he was not doing that. In fact, he told me that he was not doing anything wrong. So what was the "bad" in his life? He confessed to *feeling* tempted.

Somehow, he had it in his mind that good Christians, grown up Christians are never tempted. Temptation, to him, was a sign of failure. "Brother," I said, "the only thing your temptations prove is that there is a tempter: Satan. You are not in sin because you are tempted, you are in sin only when you give into temptation; and you have not given in! You have to keep fighting temptation just like every other believer has to keep fighting it. That's God's will."

Just as we should not be discouraged and quit regularly weeding out temptation, neither should we stop working at our quirks. Like a weight lifter who gradually adds more weight to his exercise, so the believer becomes stronger with each success over his personality weaknesses. We must learn to approach temptations and quirks with the purpose God design: to make us better Christians.

> Beloved, think it not strange concerning the fiery trial which is to try you, as though some strange thing happened unto you: But rejoice, inasmuch as ye are partakers of Christ's sufferings; that, when his glory shall be revealed, ye may be glad also with exceeding joy.
> — *1 Peter 4:12-13*

Somebody says, "Well I've been battling my flaws for a long time and I have not seemed to change." Whether *you* see

51

progress or not, God sees someone who is unwilling to lie down and accept defeat, someone who lives by faith in Christ Jesus regardless of what he feels. That pleases the Lord and that is when God releases special grace into your life. So keep swinging. After all, God loves a good fight!

Getting the Right Notion of Sin

Christians also need to know how to respond to the times when they do, in fact, fall short of God's righteousness. This is where the ride gets rough for a lot of people, so let me reach back to the first chapter and talk about the notion that "even Christians are going to continue to sin."

Many church authorities and Christian celebrities declare that a blood-washed, redeemed, child of God is *supposed to* expect iniquity in his or her life; and people blindly accept this conclusion. After all, they can look back at their own Christian walk and point out bad habits along with out-and-out failures. Then they seem to recall a Scripture—where is it?—the one that says if we say we do not sin, the truth is not in us. "That's right," they think, "Everybody sins. I've sinned as a Christian and I'm sure that I'm going to sin in the future."

Sounds right. But again, it doesn't matter what anyone else says, what is God expecting from His people? What is the Word of the Lord? This is important for us to know because it sets the tone for our behavior as well as our approach to dealing with our shortcomings. Let me take you to "that Scripture" which supposedly says that believers should confess sinfulness,

If we say that we have no sin, we deceive ourselves, and the truth is not in us. If we confess our sins, he is faithful and just to forgive us *our* sins, and to

52

cleanse us from all unrighteousness. <u>If we say that we have not sinned</u>, we make him a liar, and his word is not in us.

— 1 John 1:8-10

You may be saying to yourself, "It says it right there. Even though we are Christians, we have sin, and we should not say otherwise." Your conclusion would be correct *if that was all there was to this passage*. However, there are two qualifying verses just before:

If we say that we have fellowship with him, <u>and walk in darkness</u>, we lie, and do not the truth: <u>But if we walk in the light</u>, as he is in the light, we have fellowship one with another, and the blood of Jesus Christ his Son cleanseth us from all sin.

— 1 John 1:6-7

The context actually addresses a double standard: a confession of being in the light while walking in darkness. When this contradiction exists, God says we have no fellowship with Him, and we "deceive ourselves, and the truth is not in us." If we *continue* claiming we have done nothing wrong, our insistence becomes an accusation, a charge that God (not us) is lying.

Neither here nor anywhere in the Bible are believers prepped for a life destined with sinful ways. Nowhere does the Holy Spirit of God encourage us to forecast, defend, or make room for sin.

The only thing in Scripture even resembling an allowance for sin is found in the very next verse after the above passage:

> My little children, these things write I unto you, <u>that ye sin not</u>. And <u>if any man sin</u>, we have an advocate with the Father, Jesus Christ the righteous:
> — *1 John 2:1*

Notice the apostle John does not say "*when* any man sins" or "*because* every man sins" (and by the way, this is talking about believers, "my little children"), he says "if" and "if" is a big word. "If" categorizes sin by a believer as something unplanned, irregular, or better yet, that which should never have happened, an accident.

The foremost thing you need to know about dealing with sin and sinful habits is God expects "that ye sin not." Thankfully, God has, through Christ Jesus, made a way for believers to handle accidents; but understand the whole reason you have a heavenly Advocate in the first place is specifically because *God wants you to be sinless*.

More About the Right Notion

I have heard some preachers say that if you are really mature in the Lord, you can handle a bit of carnality and sin in your life, but that is not Jesus' way of thinking. Jesus taught that sin defiles a person and actually makes him hide from and hate the light of God.[3] Christ sees both the immediate and the long-term dangers of wrong and rebellious behavior. He knows that sin brings harm, grief, decay, corruption, and chaos; that it makes you and me vulnerable, weak, ignorant, and ineffective.

He may be presented today as being a Savior who winks at your indiscretions and lets you develop in His Kingdom at your own pace with your own options; but make no mistake, the cool, I'll-do-my-thing-you-do-your-thing dude is the wrong portrait of Jesus.

In my opinion, there is no passage more wrongfully used to repaint a laissez-faire Christ than the story of the adulteress.[4] You remember it: The Pharisees brought a woman to Jesus who had been caught in the very act of infidelity. They wanted to stone the woman, (the legitimate and legal thing to do under Levitical Law,[5]) but they brought her to Jesus first to see if He would contradict Moses. Refusing to go along with their scheme, Jesus said, "He that is without sin among you, let him first cast a stone at her," and one by one the Pharisees left, revealing that they were hypocrites, doing things as wicked as adultery and perhaps being adulterers themselves. When none of her Pharisee accusers remained, Jesus said to the woman "Neither do I condemn thee: go, and sin no more."

People take this last statement and run with it, preaching that Jesus refused to judge the adulteress, and therefore we have no right to tell others that they are sinners; but look again at what the Lord said. Jesus *did* judge, both the woman and her adultery. "Sin no more" was Jesus' verdict. Later in the book of Revelation, He warned that He was going to send "great tribulation" against adulterers.[6] As far as adultery itself, Christ did not come to *destroy* the Law against this transgression, He came to *fulfill* it. Jesus upped the standard and taught that lust, the root of the out-and-out act, was immoral, sinful, and deserving of Hell fire.

Moses was indeed a lawgiver but Jesus is the Supreme Justice, and His ruling to all those who trespass is, "Sin no more! Don't think it and don't do it!"

My Bible tells me that Jesus Christ came to take sin away,[7] to destroy it,[8] and that in Him there is no sin.[9] Do not be taken in by today's feel-good, everything's-rosy theology. In no way does Jesus promote sin.

> But if, while we seek to be justified by Christ, we ourselves also are found sinners, _is therefore Christ the minister of sin? God forbid._
>
> — _Galatians 2:17_

You can know you are growing in Christ when more and more you love what He loves _and hate what He hates._ I know that last statement will cause the spiritually out of shape to cringe; but then again, we are not talking about nursery room things, are we? Besides, the Bible very clearly states the Lord Jesus Christ, in fact, _hates_ certain things:

> But unto the Son _he saith,_ Thy throne, O God, _is_ for ever and ever: a sceptre of righteousness _is_ the sceptre of thy kingdom. Thou hast loved righteousness, _and hated iniquity;_ therefore God, _even_ thy God, hath anointed thee with the oil of gladness above thy fellows.
>
> —_Hebrews 1:8-9_

> These six _things_ doth the LORD hate: yea, seven _are_ an abomination unto him …
>
> —_Proverbs 6:16_

So hast thou also them that hold the doctrine of the Nicolaitanes, <u>which thing I hate</u>. Repent; or else I will come unto thee quickly, <u>and will fight against them</u> with the sword of my mouth.

—*Revelation 2:15-16*

Taking Jesus' side and battling for His cause shows real maturity and positions you to overcome temptation. Do not be fooled! You will never increase in your love for God if you are still flirting with the devil. You will never be able to "cleave to that which is good" if you are unwilling to "abhor that which is evil."[10] For that matter, you will never be able to save certain people "with fear, pulling them out of the fire" unless you are "hating even the garment spotted by the flesh."[11]

We must understand the purpose of Jesus' death, burial, and resurrection was to save us *from* sin, not to save us *with* sin. On the cross, Jesus traded places with us and took our condemnation, guilt, and indebtedness. Hallelujah! Yet to complete the transaction, we must take *His* place of righteousness, truth, and holiness.

For the grace of God that bringeth salvation hath appeared to all men, teaching us that, denying ungodliness and worldly lusts, we should live soberly, righteously, and godly, in this present world;

— *Titus 2:11-12*

Let me say this another way: The primary position you should take about sin is that it's a completely unacceptable condition that can only be fixed by repentance and never fixed by excuses. To expect or allow sin is to utterly misunderstand the nature of God's grace and to completely ignore Christ's aim at perfecting you. Recognize that your lapse into the unacceptable is not proof of a destined-to-sin standard in Christianity. How the devil loves to convince people otherwise! The only thing it proves is that you are not your own savior. You need a Priest, an Advocate, a Comforter who can help you return to perfection's righteous path.

* * * * *

Saying that you will probably sin in the future may sound sincere and saying are a "sinner saved by grace" may sound humble, but such confessions for Christians are nowhere in the Bible. They are perspectives that come from carnal self-evaluation, not from a position of faith. When you converted to Jesus Christ, God ceased to call you a sinner and He now calls you His son or His daughter.

To be an overcomer, to walk in godly perfection you must stop predicting personal sinfulness and start claiming Jesus' righteousness. As a disciple of Christ, your identity is not drawn from your quirks, your temptations, or your accidents. Jesus is the New Man into whom you are conforming. He, and He alone, is to be your character, your personality, and your life choices.

If you have a ladder mentality, you will strive after a magic moment when all your quirks suddenly disappear and when you *feel* like a glorified soul, but that is unrealistic and unattainable. God's solution is that you view your life as being hid in Christ, be filled with the Holy Ghost that loves righteousness, and keep overcoming sin, flesh, and the devil.

Dealing With Our Sin

The knee-jerk reaction everyone experiences after slipping up is the old Adamic three step: deny, downplay, and defend. Deny that you even did anything wrong; downplay the cost and the consequence; and defend yourself as being the real victim. The danger is this triple shuffle progressively hardens you from the conviction of the Holy Spirit; and if you continue ignoring His faithful influence, you will develop a "conscience seared with a hot iron,"[12] a severe deception when you no longer feel guilt from your committed sin and when you believe you can live in darkness yet still enjoy benefits of the light.

Something else happens right after making a mistake or committing a sin: the devil starts talking to you. Perhaps he will say, "Now that you made a slip-up, you just ruined your witness. No one is going to listen to you anymore. You'd better be quiet from now on." He might even say something like, "See! You failed again! Maybe you are not cut out to be a Christian. Maybe you were never a Christian in the first place. Maybe all this time you only *imagined* a new life, and now the real you is coming out." Waste no time in rebuking that sly serpent in Jesus' name. Keep in mind that *everything* he says is a lie. He may sound as though he is sympathizing with you, but his actual motive is to pull you down and take you out. Never accept the comfort of the devil's twisted pity.

The perfect way to handle a mistake is first to be sensitive to the prick of the Holy Spirit. Divine conviction, like physical pain, lets you know something is wrong and needs correction; and only as you properly respond to the sting of guilt can you receive the strength of God's grace. Once you have faced the truth, turn to the Lord and ask His forgiveness. Accept full responsibility for any penalties or patch-ups, liberally blame yourself, and above all make no excuses. Repentance—not denial, not depression, and not giving up—is the only right reaction to a failing. It is the only mature and satisfactory thing to do, and sinners will learn this as Christians exemplify it.

Some people, influenced by the enemy and their own conceit, feel confident that single-handedly they can fix their past failures and get the better of their present ones; but sin, like perfection, is not about how *we* see things or even how things effect *us*. Our iniquities have offended and separated us from our Maker.

> Against thee, thee only, have I sinned, and done *this* evil in thy sight.
> — *Psalms 51:4a*

After committing a wrong, we need more than the acceptance of an apology. We need mercy from God and healing in our soul. What separates healthy repentance from a selfish show of regret is when we seek to make things 100 percent right with the One who knows the secrets of our hearts; and this, too, makes an impression on the world.

> He that covereth his sins shall not prosper: but whoso confesseth and forsaketh *them* shall have mercy.
> — *Proverbs 28:13*

Sinners also need to learn from believers that God requires more from us than a quick, easy "I'm sorry." Repentance is not yard sale bartering.

Take a lesson from that crooked little tax collector in the Bible, Zacchaeus. After Jesus came to his house, he did not defend or gloss over his iniquities. He did not insist on conditional actions from the Lord or from others ("If this and that were done, I know I could be a good Christian"). He owned up to his errors and truly repented by giving back four times what he had stolen. Giving back exactly what he had stolen would have been a sign that he was sorry; but Zacchaeus sought no cheap apology for his exploitation, he was after permanent closure of his old life.

Imagine what his victims must have thought? They would have had a renewed opinion of Zacchaeus but undoubtedly would have been curious why he turned over a new leaf. Who knows how many became Jesus' followers simply because of Zacchaeus's complete repentance?

So much good happens when Christians deal with mistakes maturely and with excellence, going above and beyond to correct the situation; relationships are restored, righteousness is re-emphasized, respect is reinstated, and revival becomes ripe.

Asking for an Audit

As long as we are talking about perfection and repentance, let me add a side note. Those who are really mature in Christ Jesus will always be interested in keeping a weed-free garden; they will diligently attend to blunders and blind spots. Eager to be productive in their garden, they pray as David:

> Search me, O God, and know my heart: try me, and know my thoughts: and see if *there be any* wicked way in me, and lead me in the way everlasting.
> — *Psalms 139:23-24*

61

Yes, we must often ask the Lord for a personal audit, a divine forensic investigation simply because we tend to miss if not dodge the potentially corrupt in our lives. We need the light of Christ to keep us honest and in check.

Do not grow weary with your garden work. Quirks, mistakes, and sins are problems that must constantly be overcome, but you do not have to be burdened or identified with them. God's perfection plan *includes* the resistance of temptation and the process of repentance. Hallelujah!

* * * * *

I thank God for that old, rugged cross to which I first came and found redemption. I thank the Lord for that heavenly throne to which I now confidently come as an heir to find restored favor,[13] spiritual health, and a perfecting power. I never have to wonder or worry about my future; whether at the Last Day I am going to Heaven or to Hell. Jesus Christ has power on Earth to forgive sins, and I can know here and now that my repentance has been totally accepted.

> But the God of all grace, who hath called us unto his eternal glory by Christ Jesus, after that ye have suffered a while, <u>make you perfect</u>, stablish, strengthen, settle *you*.
>
> — *1 Peter 5:10*

CHAPTER FOUR REVIEW

1. In coming in the flesh, Jesus set the precedent for human perfection.

2. Personal quirks, like temptations, are designed to make you a better Christian. You become stronger and stronger with each victory.

3. Nowhere in the Bible does God encourage us to forecast sin, expect sin, or make room for sin.

4. God expects "that ye sin not." God has, through Christ Jesus, made a way to handle "accidents" in the Christian life; but understand, the reason you have a heavenly Advocate is because *God wants you to be sinless.*

5. Jesus ruling to all those who trespass is, "Sin no more!"

6. As a disciple of Christ, you are not to draw your identity from your quirks, your temptations, or your mistakes. Jesus is the New Man into whom you are conforming.

7. So much good happens when Christians deal with mistakes with excellence.

8. Often, we need an "audit" from the Lord to keep us honest and in check.

FIVE

The Hardest Thing to Handle

It is a test just as brutal and intense as what persecution, rejection, lack, loss, or disadvantage could ever be; a condition that has proved to be the breaking point for many a great man and many a great culture; and arguably the most consequential trial of all humanity. What is this formidable proving ground of perfection? The point and time of success.

History is littered with societies who worked their way to breathtaking greatness only to plummet to shocking futility (if not shameful extinction), their downfall marked by lawlessness, greed, and overconfidence which followed their success. Even more disturbing: Our here-and-now world is filled with individuals who started out as nobodies, beat the odds with incredible accomplishments, yet as soon as they became successful they turned into out-of-control monsters, infamous for their arrogance, cynicism, overindulgence, and corruption. We are not just talking about big time success associated with business tycoons or pop-culture stars. Whether it is fame, money, power, position, or even knowledge, people everywhere prove that whatever degree of reward or pursuit, the hardest thing to handle in life is the reality of dreams come true.

Success does not look or feel like a test because the pressure and setting are very different. Even so, most people and peoples never hold up under the weight which accomplishment and pleasure puts on their foundational values. Why? The biggest reason is, again, that old model of forbidden perfection. Those who "make it" see themselves as having reached a permanent, unchallenged, elite status, an ultimate ladder level. Neglecting God's garden ways, they fail to see the urgency of otherwise normal, wholesome continuation. It makes no difference to them what led up to their success; now that they are pursuing the novel promises of pride, their once productive principles are suddenly abandoned and left to rot.

Of Christian Success

Do not think this problem is unique to worldly things. It is possible for believers to begin "in the Spirit" yet end up "in the flesh."[1] If you doubt me, take a look in your Bible. Solomon could not handle his God-given gift of wisdom. He went into gross idolatry and forgot the Lord. The adult Israelites under Moses could not handle the many miracles that brought them freedom and sustenance. They continued complaining and distrusting, and eventually lost their lives in the wilderness. The church of Ephesus could not handle its spiritual success regardless of their significant efforts, admirable patience, and doctrinal purity; the assembly left its first love and, through John's vision, was publically rebuked by Christ who warned of removing its "candlestick."`

Yes, people have just as much of a struggle with spiritual success as with any other kind.

As a pastor I have often seen new believers enter the faith red hot for God, but then shortly after they leveled out and became cold, carnal, and even backslidden. They were clueless about where to go after God has given them their breakthrough, and therefore they lost everything they gained. I do not care what your theology is, I have seen it happen. Oh, in their dark days of trouble, they willingly surrendered and humbled themselves before the Lord, seeking out and obeying all godly counsel. With remarkable dedication, they stuck to the Word, sought the face of the Lord, and were loving and faithful to the Body of Christ. For some of them, their zeal opened the door to actually enter the ministry. As always, God graciously answered their prayers and brought them deliverance—even with some added measure of success and prosperity—but just when they were established and of the most use to the Kingdom, what did they do?

Finally liking themselves and their situation, they looked for the easy chair, the retirement check, the lukewarm days. They stopped stepping out in faith. They stopped praying, fasting, and guarding themselves against "the filthiness of the flesh and spirit." They stopped depending on divine directives and started leaning on personal performance. Fearing man more than God, they suddenly wanted to tone down their enthusiasm, make their faith user friendly, and they started talking about how religion should be a personal and a regimented thing. As time went by, they became more and more carnal, and less and less spiritual. Of coarse, they didn't see it that way because they entertained a ladder mentality and thought they had forever mastered some spiritual height. What a tragedy.

Six Secrets to Handling Success

Much of what we call success hinges on circumstances and assets, summer days we claim as our own. Yet just as summer goes away without our permission, circumstances always change and assets eventually disappear. Accumulated wealth is quickly tied up or consumed; frenzied fame has a way of suddenly migrating to someone else; even the glow of personal accomplishment hastily fades in light of new knowledge, new competition, and new goals. What then of self-worth and "making it?"

Real success should never be confused with the one-dimensional variety (money, fame, etc.), yet it almost always is. It seems that common sense and proper behavior do not come naturally to people once they have won their superficial desires. Happily, there is a way to gain experience and know-how, to enjoy peace and prosperity, to take on favor and authority, yet be as fervent, as effective, and as pure as ever before; but it means forgetting the ladder and remembering that you are in a world of sowing and reaping.

1. Keep on being thankful.

> I will remember the works of the LORD: surely I will remember thy wonders of old. I will meditate also of all thy work, and talk of thy doings.
> —*Psalms 77:11-12*

Once you have come to a place of success, beware of Satan's lie that you *deserve* to be blessed and that even God is now *obligated* to meet your needs. This only leads to complaining, to concluding the Lord has really done very little for you, and eventually to developing the dreaded "reprobate mind,"[2] a poisoned state of the soul that is darker and more rebellious than before conversion.[3] Instead, realize that all around you are situations and assets that would not exist without the hand of God. Small or big, gentle or explosive, treat all blessings coming to you with utmost appreciation, not just when you feel like it or when it makes you look good. Comparing your blessings with your neighbor's is never a wise habit, and assuming that others should give you preferential treatment is just as much ingratitude as complaining. To stay thankful, successful, and to be perfect, simply cherish what is in your hand.

2. Always factor in the possibility of personal weakness and probable error.

> God resisteth the proud, and giveth grace to the humble.
> *—1 Peter 5:5b*

> Where no counsel *is,* the people fall: but in the multitude of <u>counsellors</u> *there is* <u>safety</u>.
> *—Proverbs 11:14*

The best thing you can do is opposite of how success makes you feel: be humble. Never stop seeing your limits and never develop the stubborn notion that you are always right (or even *mostly* right). Never assume a victory and never underestimate your challenges. Never take yourself out from underneath authority or accountability. Never stop asking for good advice, never stop taking it. Never stop praying or putting your faith in the things of God, and never run ahead of the Lord's will. If you are to assume anything, assume that God is always right and you are not.

Incidentally, when a person is down and needs a breakthrough, it is good for that individual to remind himself of who he is and what he has in Christ Jesus. After the breakthrough, though, when he is walking in Heaven's blessings, it is good for that individual to remind himself of who he is not, how disadvantaged he remains, and how he is still so utterly reliant on the Creator. This is what the Bible calls being "poor in spirit," and this is where there is abundant grace and continued success.

3. Go on fighting for the truth of Jesus Christ.

> For do I now persuade men, or God? or do I seek to please men? for if I yet pleased men, I should not be the servant of Christ.
> —*Galatians 1:10*

When you become successful in something, you almost always gain favorable recognition from others. While there is no sin in being well-liked or well-known, the danger is when you begin basing your behavior on popularity rather than principle. In the Kingdom, to *keep* success means a readiness to *lose* success. In other words, if you are going to be a winner before the Lord, be ready, like Jesus, to be a loser before the world. Reputation, applause, opportunity, promotion, even survival, all of these must be disposable for the greater cause of Jesus and His truth. As a believer you are to be owned by no one but God Almighty. The only thing you are to owe others is to love them, and love enough to tell them the truth. This, too, is real and continual success.

4. Stay in fellowship with good, godly people.

And let us consider one another to provoke unto love and to good works: <u>not forsaking the assembling of ourselves together</u>, as the manner of some *is;* but exhorting *one another:* and so much the more, as ye see the day approaching.

—*Hebrews 10:24-25*

Another temptation you will have after success is to view everyone, except an elite few, as lazy ignoramuses who are wasting their life at inferior pursuits. You will be tempted to withdraw from the "lowlife;" however, the problem with all such self-imposed segregation is that you lose touch with reality and become useless, draining, and strange. You need to maintain contact with *ordinary* people, with old friends, and especially with those who are strong in the faith.

Yes, "assembling" means going to church, but by extension it means getting personally involved with people, and specifically those who need your godly exhortation and Christian "provoking." Maybe you will have to deal with bad attitudes. Maybe you will have to burn some extra gas in your car or interrupt your schedule now and again. Maybe you will occasionally have to work with individuals who smell, are uneducated, or are cruder than they should be. Do not whine, shine. When you isolate yourself to a clique of maintenance-free friends, you challenge no one in their faith, *and no one challenges you.* If you are going to stay spiritually healthy and successful, continue assembling with people. Stay touchable and you will stay alive.

5. Avoid overindulgence and making things too comfortable for yourself.

Now they [which run in a race] *do it* to obtain a
corruptible crown; but we an incorruptible. I therefore
so run, not as uncertainly; so fight I, not as one that
beateth the air: but I keep under my body, and bring it
into subjection: lest that by any means, when I have
preached to others, I myself should be a castaway.

—1 Corinthians 9:25-27

Remember, self-control means more than restraining from
this or that. It means making yourself do what is right. Just
because you have realized certain goals or have acquired certain
comforts does not mean you have can retire from life. You must
continue pushing yourself to keep the principles and purposes of
Jesus Christ. Success is a very vulnerable place to be, and you
will actually have *more* temptations to compromise and to be
prideful than ever before. Like a young athlete training to
improve his ability, you must deliberately put yourself in
situations that stretch your convictions and sharpen your faith.
Fasting with prayer is the one of the best ways of "keeping your
body under."[4] Another way is to be generous regularly with
your material things. Beware of indulging in too much luxury,
too much entertainment, and even too much food (remember,
gluttony is a sin[5]). Guard against physical laziness, avoid
exorbitant financial waste, and occasionally get some dirt under
those fingernails. Never make decisions on a pleasantness or
materialistic basis; continue to live by principles, even if it
means loosing a certain standard of living. You will never be
sorry you did.

6. Continue taking risks.

72

The slothful *man* saith, *There is* a lion in the way; a
lion *is* in the streets.

—*Proverbs 26:13*

The way of the slothful *man is* as an hedge of
thorns: but the way of the righteous *is* made plain.

—*Proverbs 15:19*

I don't think there is a nicer way to say it and still have the
same impact: The person who stops taking chances and
becomes obsessed with holding onto what he has earned is lazy.
Successful or not, when you take effort and obstacles out of
your life, your world starts to rot. Your laziness will essentially
become "an hedge of thorns;" and that simply means that unless
you stay on the offensive to gain ground, you will find yourself
on the defensive and loose ground.

You may worry, "What if I get burnt by people? What if I
make a mistake? What if I have to backtrack? I don't want to
lose what I've gained." Listen, whatever you have achieved
must not become your coffin. The Bible says that man was
"born unto trouble."[6] Hard times and threatening circumstances
are a part of life, yet God designed you to take dominion.[7]
Never become corrupt by laziness. Face life's risks and trust in
God. For the just shall live by faith.

The Ultimate Secret

Real success is something anyone can attain, something
much more permanent and fulfilling than ladder-level ideals
achieved by a privileged few. There are two scriptures that best
express this fact. Here is the first:

Godliness with contentment is great gain.

—*1 Timothy 6:6*

Man's contentment is selfish, based on how one perceives his personal circumstances, which is exactly why man's contentment is fickle, coming and going with the winds of emotion. God's contentment, however, is based on truth and reality, and is, therefore, enduring. It's the better contentment. There is no clearer proof of this than the grocery store checkout lines. Yes, the place where everyone has to face those tabloid headlines. Week after week, you can see in brilliant print what are supposed to be successful individuals, living in a dizzy world of chaos: cheating, divorce, intrigue, fighting, drug court—real-life soap operas. One month these far-from-righteous people are telling the press how happy they are; the next, they're threatening suicide. These are the heroes everyone wants to be like? These are the ones who exemplify contentment? Wrong!

Massive homes and lavish yachts cannot buy satisfaction. Head-turning recognition does not guarantee happiness. Breaking some record, winning some position, being the first to have this or that is so empty and hollow, incapable of instilling lush, invaluable contentment. I've met people who hardly have enough money to put food on the table, and yet they are perfectly rich. They have in their lives an abundance of the peace, love, and joy that comes by the Word of God. (Remember, it's the Seed!) These are the ones who are actually content and truly successful.

Here is the second verse, which takes things a bit further:

I have learned, in whatsoever state I am, *therewith* to be <u>content</u>. I know <u>both</u> how to be abased, and I know how to abound: every where and in all things I am instructed both to be full and to be hungry, both to abound and to suffer need. I can do all things through Christ which strengtheneth me.

—Philippians 4:11b-13

On one hand, contentment comes by living in the decency and order of godliness. On the other hand, it comes by accepting and cooperating with what God is doing in our lives.

Not everyone is going to be rich. Not everyone is going to be famous. Not everyone is going to have the same skills, the same opportunities, or even the same lifespan. Similarly, not everyday is going to be filled with rainbows and cotton candy. Life has coexisting highs and lows, and each of us is called by God to walk a certain path. That is why you must learn to allow Christ to strengthen you in all the avenues of your individual life and to find the real kind contentment that only comes from Him. In the Word and will of God, *there is success and satisfaction for everyone*, whether you are in a circumstance of abounding or a situation of suffering need.

Recently, a young preacher from Armenia spoke at our church and made a fascinating statement. He talked about the history of his country, how in 301 A.D. it became the first Christian nation ever; and yet how, in recent centuries, it has endured much oppression and bloodshed by surrounding Muslim countries. "Your nation," he said to us, "has been blessed because you stood for the Word of God. My country has suffered persecution because we stood for the Word of God. To God be the glory!"

* * * * *

The paradox of handling success is that *success was never meant to be handled.*

In whatever form it comes, temporal achievement is something that ultimately cannot be owned, manipulated, or assumed, for is not ours in the first place.

True, confidence is a quality for which we inherently yearn. Yet if there is a confidence into which one must mature, it is certainly not self-confidence or one that breeds secular skepticism. Therefore, while we may be conscious of nothing more than the role we play, we must recognize that it is He that sits on high who is ultimately responsible for situating us in the right place, at the right time, and with all the right ingredients. The Bible says the Lord "putteth down one, and setteth up another,"[8] that He gives "power to get wealth,"[9] and that it is through His wisdom that men "find out knowledge of witty inventions."[10]

We must view material success for what it really is: God's unmerited blessing. Yet however much or however little of that kind of blessing we have, no situation in our lives should stop us from perfect, unbroken confidence in the Lord Jesus Christ. He is our real success.

CHAPTER FIVE REVIEW

1. People have just as much of a struggle with spiritual success as with any other kind.

Keys to success ...

2. Keep on being thankful.

3. Always factor in the possibility of personal weakness and probable error.

4. Go on fighting for the truth.

5. Stay in fellowship with good, godly people.

6. Avoid overindulgence and making things too comfortable for yourself.

7. Continue taking risks.

8. Success is not something to be owned, manipulated, or assumed because success is not ours in the first place.

THE BATTERY KEY

SIX

Two Sides to Perfection

I have a battery in my car, and though it may be both unseen and unsightly, without it my vehicle could go nowhere and do nothing. I need that battery.

Now a battery has two parts to it: a positive side and a negative side. I cannot use just the positive side or just the negative side. For electricity to be generated, both must function together.

The things of God are the same. There is a positive, exhilarating, and blessing side; and there is a negative, sobering, and dreadful side.

God Himself operates in both the positive and the negative, and thus He is complete, whole, and well-rounded. He is perfect. God loves, but He also hates.[1] He makes alive, but He also kills.[2] He is the Prince of Peace,[3] but He is also a Man of War.[4] God is "all, and in all."[5] If you are going to be complete, mature, and perfect you need to see things God's way, even if it is very different from your point of view.

How many theologians and denominations, failing to consider God's paradoxes, have tended to favor only one side of a Bible doctrine and practically ignore the other. When all their fancy words and emphatic illustrations are ended, the fact is that imbalanced doctrine can be just as bad as outright false doctrine. Lopsided, conflict-ridden theology has a history of damaging Christian unity and triggering disconnect in the lives of believers. Sadly, many who go to church remain shallow, are unnecessarily taken advantage of, settle for second-rate effectiveness, and suffer pointless personal conflicts, all because they try to make life work by good-meaning yet one-sided notions some preacher sold them. This should not be.

The great imbalance of our times is the attempt to ignore, discount, and even deny the negative side of the Kingdom. Preachers desperately avoid talking about Hell, divine judgment, or making serious sacrifices. The theory is that the positive side will singularly generate all the power needed. Therefore, everything is presented as "God wants to bless you. God loves you. God has a plan for you." All of this, of course, is true, but it is not the whole battery. Now, after years of being in use, this upbeat-only emphasis has produced a generation that is immature and carnal in their walk.

I grew up in church, but never have I met so many church people who, in recent years, have confessed to me that they either were or still are angry with God. Angry? The creature is angry with the Creator? How foolish! Yet because they have been programmed with a skewed it's-all-about-me gospel, these dysfunctional churchgoers walk around thinking that God exists just to assist them, that their every prayer deserves to be answered, and that they are so special that they are irreplaceable.

I say, by the unction of the Holy Ghost, it is time for battery perfection. It is time for the whole Gospel and the whole counsel of God. Yes, there is the positive of prosperity, but there is the negative of giving things up too. There is a part that announces heavenly blessings, but there is a part that warns of divine wrath. There is an aspect where it is "not of works lest any man should boast;"[6] but there is also an aspect when you "work out your own salvation with fear and trembling."[7]

Of Seasons and Times

Solomon had the revelation of positive and negative thousands of years ago. He made the observation that "to everything there is a season, and a time to every purpose under the heaven."[8] Look at all the things he listed as being seasons and times in life. Notice the positives along side the negatives:

A time to be born, and a time to die;
a time to plant, and a time to pluck up *that which is* planted;
a time to kill, and a time to heal;
a time to break down, and a time to build up;
a time to weep, and a time to laugh;
a time to mourn, and a time to dance;
a time to cast away stones, and a time to gather
stones together;
a time to embrace, and a time to refrain from embracing;
a time to get, and a time to lose;
a time to keep, and a time to cast away;
a time to rend, and a time to sew;
a time to keep silence, and a time to speak;
a time to love, and a time to hate;
a time of war, and a time of peace.

— *Ecclesiastes 3:2-8*

Solomon noted that a wise man "discerneth" or perceives what season and time it is.[9] In other words, the wise or perfect person knows what to do and when to do it.

In our church, for example, we restrict children from running in the building after service. We do not say that running is a sin just to get the kids to slow down (that is sanctimonious perfection). We simply realize that little ones racing through the crowd is inappropriate. Wrong season. Wrong time. Yet when we are at a church picnic, we do not see it as hypocrisy to encourage those same children to run, run, run. We understand they need the exercise and being outside is the season and time for running.

This is perfection.

Nonetheless, people often and unfortunately want to deny certain seasons of life even exist (e.g., it is never right to run). Either they want to close their eyes to things they find unpleasant, inconvenient, and complex or they do not intend on considering anything outside their hasty assumptions. Sanctimonious people are notorious for this; yet such ignorance is imperfect and not God.

Jesus taught us that we are to be perfect just as Father is perfect.[10] That is right! God wants us, His Church, to be well-rounded, fully developed, and grow up in all truth and righteousness in this life. Carelessness, gullibility, lack of insight, and incompetence in decision-making are characteristics for which we should not settle. God operates in the full power of wisdom, and He calls us to do the same.

No, God does not endorse the "openness" of humanism, which claims that there is no right or wrong and that practically every action of man is acceptable. There is a gauge to wisdom, knowledge, and good judgment: the Lord Himself. It is within

His context of truth that God wants us to take everything into consideration, test both sides of the battery, discern where the truth is, and act on it.

Perfection and maturity, then, mean seeking God, constantly praying, "Lord, what is appropriate here in this situation? What is Your will, Your Word at this moment? What side of the battery are You working through right now?"

Most of the time, discerning the right season and doing the right thing will be completely opposite from what you think and feel; but again, God's will is your unit of measure. His Word and His Spirit will guide you through those tricky seasons when doing the right thing seems to contradict the circumstances.

Look at how Jesus addressed Revelation's seven churches. He started off with praise, "I know thy works," then to some He went on to say, "But I have a few things against thee." It was not all positive, it was not all negative, but in the same conversation Jesus had perfect discernment of seasons and times. He recognized everything that was happening and He spoke all that was true and right.

Here is another example. Jesus commanded us to love our enemies,[11] yet He never instructed that we should be without enemies. No matter what you do in life—even if it is good and right—you will always have people who hate you and people with whom you must disagree. Jesus was teaching us that *within the circumstance of conflict* there are seasons and times when you must be affectionate toward and benevolent to those with whom you are at odds. Your act of love may prove to have no resolving impact upon them whatsoever; they may still harbor contempt against you and you may still have to oppose things in their life. Yet as a Christian, you are to be always fair and civil.

Anyone can live by their feelings, and most people do. Yet if in this world we are going to be full and perfect lights for Christ, we need to deal with the bitter and the sweet, the difficult and the easy, the rubber-meets-the-road stuff with all our Third Heaven revelations. The good news is, this is something all of us, through Christ Jesus, can learn to do.

No Cure-alls

Let me take this battery key one step farther. Have you ever seen an advertisement for one of those breakthrough diets on TV or in a magazine? It seems that most of them go something like this:

> This diet is guaranteed to burn off a pound an hour, and the amazing thing is it is not just for weight loss! It clears up your sinuses too! It lubricates your joints. It restores memory loss, hearing loss, and hair loss. It even reverses the aging process. Yes sir! This miracle diet does everything, and just look at all the movie stars that are endorsing it. All of them encourage you to buy into our program so that you never have any more worries. Wow!

If you have been around for a bit, you know that a pitch like this is a stretch of the truth. OK, maybe the diet really would be good for losing a few pounds and for adding some vitamins to your regimen. But to claim the product as a cure-all is both dishonest and unrealistic.

When it comes to conduct, outlook, and even faith, most people would rather search the world for quickie cure-alls than learn how to discern seasons and times. For instance, suppose someone has had a real, genuine, life-changing experience with learning how to laugh. Now, that person has a passion for getting others to learn to laugh. That is fine. What frequently happens, though, is the individual will step over the line and begin presenting their particular experience or insight as being the answer to all problems all the time. In this case, laughter would become the cure-all.

It is fantasy to think that life is about cure-alls, shortcuts, or your preferred side of the battery. Life simultaneously operates by multiple and seemingly opposite attributes. Laughing is good, but crying can be good too. Tolerance is good, but so is justice. Encouragement is good, but correction is good as well. When you try to control life via a one-size-fits-all formula, you become easy to fool and quick to fall.

Wisdom is what you need, but wisdom is not a property (such as gravity) nor is it the expertise of the expert. Wisdom is a Being. The Bible says that Christ Jesus is "made unto us wisdom."[12] When you follow your own prescriptions for life, you assume the place of divinity and thereby shut your ears to God's faithful and true guidance that is in Jesus. Forget an attractive yet impersonal cure-all in life; you need the living Jesus. He is the Battery, the Wisdom you must plug into for know-how; and you are not to control Him, He is to control you.

People may get annoyed with me for this but it is true and needs to be said. Churches often identify themselves by some kind of cure-all. I have heard pastors say, "We're a faith church," "This is a praise church," or "We're a user-friendly church." This kind of nonsense is just what was going on in the first century. Some people were saying, "I'm of Paul." Others were saying, "I'm of Cephas." Then there was, "I'm of Apollos."[13] Everyone was lining up behind his favorite ministry and declaring that he had it just a little bit better than the rest. Well if that kind of behavior was immature, carnal, and deserving of rebuke *then,* it still is *today!*

We have but one Lord, one faith, one Spirit, one baptism, and one way of obtaining divine Wisdom—it is by and through the Lord Jesus Christ. That is the Father's design. At some point, religious cure-alls will always contradict and depart from God's perfection. Such is the nature of all man-made, man-controlled things. Therefore, to be mature and truly free, we cannot invest our loyalty in anything less than Christ Jesus. We must confess Him as our single secret to wholeness.

> Now the God of peace ... <u>make you perfect</u> in every good work to do his will, <u>working in you</u> that which is well pleasing in his sight, <u>through Jesus Christ</u>; to whom *be* glory for ever and ever. Amen.
> — *Hebrews 13:20-21*

Learn to recognize what God is doing in your life and how He is leading you. Sometimes, He will deal with you in ways that are very pleasing to you, but other times in ways that are very intense. Sometimes He will bring sunshine and flowers, but other times clouds and cold. Pay attention and follow Him patiently because every place to which He leads you is necessary.

Another thing, and I know this is unpopular, God will do more than prosper and bless you. In the right season, at the right time, He will also correct you, but He says, "As many as I love, I rebuke and chasten."[14]

Learn to be thankful for and cooperative in these negative seasons of reprimand, and learn to be just as loyal and sold out in them too. They are important in bringing balance. Your freedom must be enriched by discipline. Your confidence must be tempered by humility. Your authority must be seasoned with surrender. In both positive and negative, encouragement and punishment, God is working and empowering you toward perfection.

> If ye endure chastening, God dealeth with you as with sons ... now no chastening for the present seemeth to be joyous, but grievous: nevertheless afterward it yieldeth the peaceable fruit of righteousness unto them which are exercised thereby.
>
> *— Hebrews 12:7, 11*

Is *your* battery working?

CHAPTER SIX REVIEW

1. Like a battery, the things of God have a positive side and a negative side, *and both sides are necessary.*

2. Churches today are ignoring, discounting, and even denying the negative side of the Kingdom, but this is not the whole battery.

3. A wise or perfect person must discern the "seasons and times" by constantly asking the Lord, "What is appropriate in this situation?"

4. Life simultaneously operates by multiple and seemingly opposite attributes, not by "cure alls."

5. To bring balance into your life, the Lord uses negative seasons, so appreciate them.

SEVEN

Of Fear And Love

There are three positive-versus-negative debates going on in the present-day Church that need to stop. There is the Word versus the Spirit conflict, the Heaven versus Earth conflict, and the love versus fear conflict, which I want to address first. Instead of using the battery principle and discerning seasons and times, people are needlessly taking sides and fighting against each other. I said it before and I say it again, it is time to grow up, accept the whole Word of God, and move on to more important battles.

Something you hear a lot in Church these days is, "I don't want to serve God out of fear. I only want to serve God out of love." Wow, that sounds great, so humble, so pleasant, so intelligent. Too bad it is unbiblical and unbalanced.

Eleven times in the New Testament alone we are outright *commanded* to fear the Lord.[1] Yes, love is definitely part of our worship and motives (I will talk about that later in this chapter), but fear—the negative side, the side of God's judgment and temporal and eternal wrath—is part of the Gospel too. Without healthy, godly fear, you have a non-working battery, a biased faith that effectively contradicts the fullness of Christ Jesus.

The God of grace, under a covenant of grace, still expects the awe and discretion that has always been owed to His holiness. The pages of the New Testament reveal that the Never-changing One continues to curse the rebel,[2] punish the uncooperative,[3] and refuse the prayers of the disobedient.[4] God will never jeopardize the integrity of His Word. He refuses to be taken lightly and He will not be questioned, manipulated, or put to the test, even by the children He loves. In other words, there are reasons to love God, but there are reasons to fear Him as well.

> And now, Israel, what doth the LORD thy God require of thee, but <u>to fear the LORD thy God</u>, to walk in all his ways, and <u>to love him</u>, and to serve the LORD thy God with all thy heart and with all thy soul,
> — *Deuteronomy 10:12*

> Wherefore we receiving a kingdom which cannot be moved, let us have grace, whereby we may <u>serve God acceptably with reverence and godly fear: for our God *is* a consuming fire.</u>
> — *Hebrews 12:28-29*

Danger of Not Fearing

What happens if you have no fear? Take a look at children. Because they have no sense of fear they will unwisely pick up, and sometimes eat, poison, put a plastic bag over their head, or perhaps play in the middle of the road. How about the unauthorized person who manages to wander onto a job site? Being oblivious to the dangers around him, he has no fear, so he reaches into a "hot" electric box or strikes a match near flammable chemicals. I once heard a biker say, "The day you trust your motorcycle, is the day you need to put it away." His point was that when you stop having a sense of fear, you are in greater danger of an accident.

When the Church refuses to accept that God gets angry and when it fails to warn that God is constantly assessing man's actions (rewarding and punishing both now and in eternity), two things happen. First, the general population becomes ignorant of the consequences of sin. Second, there is a subsequent outbreak of bold, blasphemous, in-your-face debauchery. In other words, sinners brag of picking up poison and saints run to play in the middle of the road. Without a fear of God, all of society accelerates with shocking speed toward self-annihilation.

> A wise *man* feareth, and departeth from evil: but the
> fool rageth, and is confident.
>
> — *Proverbs 14:16*

What Fear is Cast Out?

If fear is commanded in the New Testament, and if fear and love are paralleling requirements, then what did the apostle John mean in the following and often quoted verse?

> There is no fear in love; but perfect love casteth out
> fear: because fear hath torment. He that feareth is
> not made perfect in love.
>
> — *1 John 4:18*

By isolating this one passage, some make the case that we should, in fact, disregard any fear of God and just love Him. Yet when you recall what Christ and the apostles taught, John included, (for it was he who penned, "Fear God" in the book of Revelation[5]), you know *that* conclusion is wrong. Still, the question begs to be answered: What fear is "cast out" by love? The answer is found in the surrounding verses:

> No man hath seen God at any time. <u>If we love one another</u>, God dwelleth in us, and his love is perfected in us ... And we have known and believed the love that God hath to us. God is love; and <u>he that dwelleth in love</u> dwelleth in God, and God in him. Herein is our love made perfect, <u>that we may have boldness in the day of judgment</u>: because as he is, so are we in this world. There is no fear in love; but perfect love casteth out fear: because fear hath torment. He that feareth is not made perfect in love. We love him, because he first loved us. <u>If a man say, I love God, and hateth his brother, he is a liar</u>: for he that loveth not his brother whom he hath seen, how can he love God whom he hath not seen?
>
> — *1 John 4:12, 16-20*

John's quick repetitive statements are a little hard to follow here, but he makes, in fact, a powerful point. He reveals that since you have "known and believed" the love of God toward you, you should realize that "God is love." You should also realize that God loves others just as He loves you; therefore, if you are to love God, *you must love others*. To say "I love God" while hating your brother makes you a liar. Without dwelling in love for both God and others, John makes it clear that you will fail to have assurance "in the day of judgment."

So, what fear is cast out by love? Not submissive carefulness before the Lord, but the "torment" of your heart condemning you of your sin and of having a disturbed and uneasy conscience before God, a conscience which would otherwise make you confident[6] at Judgment Day.

As a pastor, I have repeatedly discovered those who are constantly distressed with a gnawing fear of Hell also have private, pet sins—present or past—which they refuse to relinquish. Whether they are trying to take care of their corruption their own way or whether they want to keep the door open to future activity, they have no peace from the Holy Ghost, who constantly convicts and convinces our hearts with what is sin, righteousness, and divine decision.[7] Finding no definitive relief, they are double-minded, and as Peter wrote, "the face of the Lord *is* against them."[8] The only cure these people have for the dread on their life is unconditional surrender, single-minded obedience, and a conforming faith in Jesus. *Then* will their love for God be perfected; *then* will they find divine peace and affirmation.

When Fear is Good

Like perfection, our concept of the fear of God is disproportionate, a defective reverence easily identified because it brings paralysis and oppression, not lively faith; nevertheless, it is the only kind of religious fear most people know. It must be stopped, that is true, but not by teaching the other extreme (e.g., that Christians should sense no fear of God). Attempting a counter balance in this way, though sincere in motive, still misses the target of bringing God's people to wholeness.

There is good and healthy fear. A mother's sense of fear causes her to guard and protect her children. A hunter's sense of fear causes him to use certain safety procedures when he handles his rifle. A pedestrian's sense of fear causes him to remove sharp, protruding objects from a pathway that could injure others. For people of an unstable nation, their sense of fear causes them to develop improvements such as good government, sound laws, and a strong military.

Everyday, the right kind of fear proves to be a beneficial and productive quality. Your new car has anti-lock brakes, air bags, and seat belts. These are safety features installed to prevent a situation we fear. The otherwise odorless, natural gas you use in your home has a detectable scent additive This, too, is an indirect product of fear. The special food packaging in your grocery store, the metal detector in your airport, the antibiotic in your pharmacy, the anti-virus program on your computer, these and thousands of other wonderful, modern products were invented from a stimulus of fear.

Here is another important point: Jesus Christ is Savior and Master, and you must fully accept Him as both. Everyone likes Jesus the Savior, but unless you submit to Jesus the Master you can never be saved.[9] As much as you must receive His mercy, you must equally comply with His kingship. He has the right to tell you what to do. Saying, "I don't want to serve God out of fear," basically translates as, "I don't want to be pressured into following the Lord. I want to serve God *because I feel like it*." To the Lord, this motive is completely unacceptable. It is a direct challenge to His authority. It is rebellion in the raw.

Kind and giving as He is, there are rules and commands by which King Jesus expects you to abide; and you had better have some healthy fear in you, lest you wander from the security of His will.

> To this *man* will I look, *even* to *him that is* poor and of a contrite spirit, <u>and trembleth at my word</u>.
> — *Isaiah 66:1-2*

When Christians discriminate against the negative, when they ignorantly say, "The Gospel means 'good news' so I don't preach bad news," they are denying a complementing, or rather, a perfecting side to the Kingdom. The fear of God keeps you safe—safe from sin, the devil, and the consequences of selfish living.

You need to fear! Fear compromise, fear laziness, fear apathy, fear excess, and above all, have a fear of grieving the Holy Spirit. Keep in mind that the fear or conviction that follows a guilty conscience (as I wrote in chapter 4) is a healthy thing. It is the Lord's alarm system that goes off when something requires immediate attention, and it can actually save your life.

Together, the love and the fear of God make a powerful chemistry, and it works like this: When I was young and living in my parents' home, there were times I obeyed because I did not want to get in trouble. I feared a spanking. Other times, I obeyed because I knew it was the right thing to do. I wanted to please my parents and was thus expressing love. Together, both fear and love produced obedience through me, and my obedience contributed to the overall peace and harmony of the home.

Fear can actually be a direct byproduct of love. Look at Moses, Elijah, David, and the apostolic writers. At one time or another, each expressed a personal concern about stepping over the line and trespassing onto what offends God. Yet their apprehensions were shaped by their undeniable love for the things of the Lord. All of them protected and guarded the Anointing in their life, and their carefulness only made them more powerful.

Action and Love

If people have an imbalanced idea of godly fear, is it possible that they also have just as imperfect a notion of godly love? The answer is, yes.

In our Western culture with its romantic traditions, love is strongly equated with emotion. This is true for our relationships and nearly every other area where the word *love* would be applied. Love is, however, more than a feeling, more than a positive-only power; love itself is a battery that has a negative side, the side called *action*.

Look at the businessman who is introduced to the game of golf. A couple of his friends take him to a course and at first he is awkward. His buddies give him some tips: "Stand like this. Hold your club like that. Tilt your head this way." He hits a bit better. Following the game, he schedules another round and then buys a golf magazine. After a few more times out, he purchases his own clubs and cleat shoes, starts going to the driving range once or twice a week, actually watches golf on TV, and goes out of his way to talk to other golfers about their game. Know what is happening? The guy is developing a love for golf.

Look at the young couple that has just met. He introduces himself, she does the same. They are both smiling and being friendly, and they both have questions about the other: "Does she find me attractive?" and "I wonder what he is like?" The boy responds to a sudden impulse by inviting her out, the girl enthusiastically says, "Yes." Soon they are calling each other, having meals together, meeting each others families, telling each other their secrets, and so forth. Next thing you know, the couple find deep feelings for one another, and announce that they wish to begin making wedding plans. What are we seeing? The couple is progressing into a serious love relationship.

Let me ask you: Was the business man required to have a feeling about golf *before* he got involved with the game? No! Was the couple ready to demonstrate sentiments of marital commitment to each other *prior to* their first meeting? Of course not! As we have seen, the action of love, in fact, precedes the feeling of love. Additionally, it is the action of love that grows the feelings of love.

About Feelings

Feelings are funny things. One day they come to you all bright and sunny, the next day they are pouring rain. Up and down, strong and weak, happy and sad, they change for no apparent reason. All too often, they mock the conscience, hijack reason, and get you into more trouble than you could imagine. Like a naughty little dog, they never obey when you try to show them off and they seem to run away at every chance they get; yet, at the end of the day, they curl up next to you and give you a loyal and adorable assurance as if the world were made up of candy sprinkles.

Feelings. We can appreciate them, we can use them, we *have to* live with them, but they must *never* control us. As overcoming Christians, our feelings are important but they will always have secondary significance to acting on the Word. That is good to know. You do not necessarily have to feel in order to do. Actors learn how to project emotions without feeling them. Doctors learn how to handle emergency situations regardless of what is going on personally. Marines learn how to focus on a goal while overriding their emotions. It is the same with the things of God.

> For we walk by faith, not by sight.
> — *2 Corinthians 5:7*

There are many times in our walk that we will experience unpleasant feelings or even no feelings. Yet it is in the hard times, the sad times, and the testing times when we learn what love really is. It's like a verse from an old Ira Stanphill song that my dad occasionally sings:

> Anyone can sing when the sun's shining bright,
> But you need a song in your heart at night.

I am going to warn you right now the devil will come to you and say, "You hypocrite! You phony! You are doing what you don't feel like doing. You are smiling, but you really want to pout. You are being polite, but you really want to punch that guy. You don't want to give that money to those poor people; you know that you would rather put it in the bank." Then he will turn the tables and say something like, "Remember, God can see your heart. Why don't you 'get real' and wait until you have the proper feelings?" Again, you need to rebuke that old, lying serpent in Jesus' name! He is trying to trap you into trusting your emotional thermometer instead of putting love into action.

Do first, feel second.

Working Love

When people talk about loving God, most of the time they are thinking backwards, trying to drum up intimate emotions of devotion before having any significant interaction with the Lord. Many, in fact, have great enthusiasm; but because they fail to include right action, their zeal lacks wisdom, their faith is without substance, and eventually their dedication deteriorates. For example, should the golfer begin neglecting his game or should the couple stop communicating, love, with all its real indications, would fall apart. Though there may even be a lingering residue of sentiment, ideal conditions would be a thing of the past.

So it is with the love of God: *lack of recurring participation will corrupt passion and priority* just as fast and just as much as if bad feelings existed.

Some believe that Christians are released from doing any kind of action, that mental acknowledgement is all one needs to please God and to love Him. For them, acts or works of righteousness are little more than upgrade options for the spiritually gifted, niceties that admittedly make life easier but unnecessary for worship. Well, that is simply wrong. That is choosing one side of the battery over the other.

While the Scriptures teach that we do not work to earn salvation, those same Scriptures command us to do good works, that is, take action *as well as* have faith[10] (and by the way, faith is considered a work[11]).

For by grace are ye saved through faith; and that <u>not</u> <u>of yourselves</u>: *it is* the gift of God: <u>not of works</u>, lest any man should boast. For we are <u>his workmanship</u>, created in Christ Jesus <u>unto good works</u>, which God hath before ordained that we should walk in them.

—*Ephesians 2:8-10*

The actions that do not save are those "of yourselves," self-designed and pointing to you.[12] The actions that do save are those of God's design, those "before ordained." These are the "works" that testify of the Lord Jesus Christ, glorify your Father in Heaven, and *perfect* your love for God.

Someone says, "Hey, you're preachin' about earning your way to Heaven." No, sir! It is like the guy who walks around my town wearing army clothes, carrying army gear, talking army talk, *but he is not in the army.* Unless you are enlisted (saved), your good works mean nothing. After you sign your name with the pen of faith, you *will* do the good works "which God hath before ordained that we should walk in them."[13]

If only preachers would get together on this matter! There is no reason to take a works side or a grace side. The works of God accompany the grace of God and *vice versa.* Lord, help us to use the battery key to turn on some much needed unity.

Let me give you some practical application here. We know that if you do not love your "brother" whom you have seen, it is impossible to love God whom you have not seen;[14] but what does it mean to love "the brethren?" Does it mean maintaining feelings or reaching a mental state? I can tell you that having brotherly love goes far beyond the buzz one gets when singing unity songs with thousands of people as an electric piano plays in the background. Love becomes reality in daily, unromantic things. Forget goose pimples and a religious rush, love is directly related to, reflected in, and effected by things such as:

* How you behave toward your husband or your wife.

* Your relationship with your parents and siblings.

* The way you treat authority figures such as parents, teachers, employers, those who represent the law, and even your pastor.

* Your generosity and hospitality, or lack thereof.

* What you do when others oppose you.

* The attitude that characterizes you to friends, neighbors, coworkers, and even that slow waitress.

* How much of a Christian example you are to the world and especially to the church.[15]

The proof of your love for Jesus Christ is *after* Sunday service and *after* personal devotions. The proof is in the ordinary things, your actions. Put it this way, God is not looking for a *mood* from you, He wants to see some *movement*. He wants to see you live the love you claim to have. The paradox is, after you have showed obedient love toward God and sacrificial love toward others, you will experience a love far greater than any you have ever known.

That ye, being rooted and grounded in love, may be able to comprehend with all saints what *is* the breadth, and length, and depth, and height; and to know the love of Christ, which passeth knowledge.
— *Ephesians 3:17-19*

Fear and love. Both are more than emotions, both have a positive and a negative function, and both work together to give you and me a complete picture of Jesus—and Jesus is who we need in order to be perfect.

CHAPTER SEVEN REVIEW

1. The Bible commands us to fear the Lord. Without healthy, godly fear, you have an imperfect and lopsided revelation of Jesus.

2. When the Church has no fear of God, all society is put in danger of self-annihilation.

3. Love does not "cast out" submissive fear toward the Lord but rather the tormenting fear of a guilty conscience.

4. The right kind of fear proves to be a beneficial and productive quality.

5. Fear can actually be a byproduct of love.

6. In our Western culture, love is equated with emotion, when actually love develops through actions taken.

7. Lack of recurring action will corrupt passion and priority just as fast and just as much as if bad feelings existed.

8. Actions of God's design are "works" that testify of the Lord Jesus Christ, glorify your Father in Heaven, and *perfect* your love for God.

EIGHT

The Word and the Spirit

S uppose you are in the preparation stage of building a house. One day you get a call from your architect and he asks you this question, "So, which do you want for your home: a roof or electricity?" What would be your response? Both, of course! You would think this question *and* this architect to be really weird.

This is the same way God responds to Christian assemblies who take sides and want to be either a Bible church or a Spirit-filled church. Both sound doctrine and spiritual manifestations are part and parcel to coming "unto a perfect man, unto the measure of the stature of the fullness of Christ."[1] To choose one or the other is abnormal. It is wrong use of the battery.

I repeat, the greatest need of today's church is to get a full revelation of the Lord Jesus Christ. He both taught doctrine *and* performed miracles. He both declared His commandments *and* delegated His power. He is both the Sower of the Word[2] *and* the Baptizer of the Holy Ghost.[3]

Remember when the woman with an "issue of blood" touched Jesus and was healed?[4] It is interesting the King James

Version says "virtue" went out of Jesus for the woman's healing. Other versions use the word "power" but both are right. The Greek word *dunamis* means "strength, power, ability," and it also means "moral power and excellence of soul."[5] The woman reached for Jesus' miracle power (the Spirit), touched on Jesus' moral power (the Word), and when both came together she was more than touched in her body. Jesus said that she was made "whole."

If you are going to be whole or perfect, you must accept both the Spirit and the Word of Christ. You need more than a touch from Jesus, but you need more than a teaching from Him also. You need everything Christ is and everything He offers.

The Necessity of the Spirit

It is easy for those in the Bible camp to point the finger at some rowdy, problematic people in the Spirit-filled camp[6] and say, "See, that's why I don't believe in what they're doing." Friend, I declare to you in the name of Jesus that having the baptism in the Holy Ghost, as illustrated in the book of Acts, is absolutely essential for a full and steady walk of faith—despite bad examples.

One cannot honestly read the New Testament record without observing the first-century church had a dynamic interaction with God. The apostles were mistaken as drunks on Pentecost day because something was happening. The sick were lined up in the streets for healing because something was happening. The Roman world was turned upside down[7] because the Gospel "came not ... in word only, but also in power, and in the Holy Ghost."[8] Something was happening!

This Gospel is meant to make something happen, to bring tangible experience as well as inner belief.

Paul talked about "the power that worketh in us;"[9] but was he only referring to religious data bouncing around in our brains? Absolutely not! He was talking about the presence and power of God that is felt, seen, and known by both believer and sinner.

You will never know the Word so well as when you become baptized in the Holy Ghost. There are many things in Scripture that simply make no sense at all until you live through them by the Spirit. This is why there are scholars who know the Bible inside and out, in Hebrew and in Greek, yet they are unconverted, unbelieving, and as carnal as the devil. They know the ink and paper, but they have never gotten hold of the Spirit.

Do not be afraid of God's supernatural moving and never let the devil or a "religious spirit" rob you of what Jesus wants to give. Forget who is not doing this or who is doing that, look to the Baptizer. You can trust Him. The Word and the Spirit go together, and as long as you keep walking in Christ you do not have to be afraid of becoming heretical or cultish. Oh, you might shake, fall down, speak with tongues, and prophesy; but when such manifestations are authentically inspired by the Holy Ghost they are decent and in order,[10] God's order. They will result in right living and right revelation.

Spiritual Abuse and the Jeremiah Revelation

Here is a biblical principle that will help clarify some "Spirit-filled" issues. Jeremiah lived in a day when being a straight-shooting, full-of-integrity prophet was out of vogue. People tried to operate in the Spirit without living out the Word.

There was a sickening number of high-profile ministers going around saying, "Thus saith the Lord," and, "God showed me such and such," when really they were prophesying out of their own souls. Many "church" people of Jeremiah's day were completely out of order.

If Jeremiah was who I think he was, he probably reached a point, like many of us have in our time, when he had enough of all the garbage that was being done in the name of the prophetic. I think he very well could have he said in that sincere heart of his, "If this is prophecy, then I am against it! And even if I have something from the Lord, I don't want to say that I have a prophecy because I don't want to be identified with all the phonies." This reaction, though coming from a right motive, would have been the wrong way of dealing with his crisis.

Whether Jeremiah actually thought those things is anybody's guess. What we do know is the way in which Jeremiah was to response to the false prophets and their false prophecies.

> The prophet that hath a dream, let him tell a dream; and he that hath my word, let him speak my word faithfully. <u>What *is* the chaff to the wheat?</u> saith the LORD. *Is* not my word like as a fire? saith the LORD; and like a hammer *that* breaketh the rock in pieces?
> — *Jeremiah 23:28-29*

People who want to do what is right and who love the truth of the Word often respond to artificial, abrasive, and excessive things that are being done in the name of the Lord, specifically wrong use of supernatural gifts, with wrong behavior. Instead of using battery discernment, they allow fear or rage to rule their thinking and seek the convenient but careless solution: shut down the *practice* rather than outdo the *problem*. By taking the opposite side of the gifts, they unconsciously create another wrong extreme.

You do not stop using electricity just because you come across a bad outlet or stop driving cars just because you have been in an accident. No. It is the same with operating in the supernatural things of God.

As in Jeremiah's day, God is not blind. He sees that there are people using prophecy and other gifts for their own good; yet even during the abuse, He still wants to do supernatural things through His children.

So the Lord asks, "What does the wheat—the real Kingdom things—have to do with the chaff—the fake, the uncalled for, the out-of-order things?" The answer is: nothing! For this reason, the Lord says that true prophets should keep prophesying, true dreamers should keep telling their dreams, and true people of the Spirit should keep moving in the Spirit. I am here to tell you that the authentic "thus saith the Lord" will win out in the end anyway. Just because there is a scourge of money-hungry, trouble-making imposters running around in the Church, do not personally resist the manifestations of God's power or become cynical toward the works of Christ. Keep the power, fix the problems, and put the practice to proper use!

Like my brother, Mark, who is also a preacher, says sometimes in his sermons, "Some may abuse it, but I'm gonna use it."

Foolish Handling

Now let's talk about the other side. God never meant the experience of Pentecost to be equated with Kingdom mavericks whose risqué and bizarre lives resemble a soap opera, but that is exactly what we see today. Some of the most obnoxious and unspiritual people in the Body of Christ, parading their arrogance and error all over the world, recklessly failing in the most basic of Christian duties (such as maintaining a good marriage or properly raising their children), are those professing to be Spirit-filled. This ought not to be!

My family has been in and around the moving of the Holy Ghost for more than 100 years now, and I can tell you that whenever people receive the Baptism yet neglect the Word in their life, there will be disaster. We have seen Pentecostals and Charismatics of every stripe and color who get off—really off!—because they believe their new revelation or mind-blowing experience trumps any liability to Scripture.

I am going to let you in on a little secret: *when you forget the Seed, you will grow the weeds.* Lack of godly character is why so many incredible movements, meetings, and men are cut short of their potential. The weeds that were passed off as being insignificant shoot up bigger and faster than expected, and suddenly they dominate. Whatever good has come from the move of the Spirit soon becomes overgrown with heresy, extremism, moral failings, money problems, or some other carnal allowance. This is as sad as it is bad.

Jesus warned:

Many will say to me in that day, Lord, Lord, have
we not prophesied in thy name? and in thy name
have cast out devils? and in thy name done many
wonderful works? And then will I profess unto
them, I never knew you: depart from me, ye that
work iniquity. Therefore <u>whosoever heareth these
sayings of mine, and doeth them</u>, I will liken him
unto a wise man, which built his house upon a rock:

— Matthew 7:22-24

Who are those who "work iniquity," who disobey the "sayings"
of Christ? The same who think their gifts or their times in the
glory nullify their ungodly conduct. Claiming a Spirit-filled
experience, they lack the Spirit-filled Word; and Jesus says it
will cost them eternity.

Let me interject something here: God is pouring out His
Spirit on all flesh, giving out a gift that is free and that sets
people free. Those who are new to the things of the Spirit
(especially if they come from backgrounds of churchy
traditions, religious superstitions, doctrinal imbalances, and the
rest) find in their Baptism a freedom and a sense of freedom
they could never have imagined previously. Praise the Lord!
Yet during this mighty, fresh flow of power, these newcomers
(along with everyone else) must realize two very simple things:

1. The Holy Spirit never comes to confirm you; He comes to
   confirm the Lord Jesus Christ. The baptism is not about
   your goodness, it is about God's.

2. Whatever gifts God manifests through you are ultimately for
   the benefit of others and of the Kingdom, not for self-

promotion (you may a talking donkey but you are still a donkey[11]).

Too many people are unaware of the full implications of opening themselves up to God and His Pentecostal fire. Do not get me wrong, I love the moving of the Holy Ghost, but it is a baptism that is not to be taken lightly. Just because God manifests gifts through you or brings miracles to you or showers you with a sense of love and grace, is no sign that you can keep doing what you have always been doing or thinking like you have always been thinking. The baptism in the Holy Ghost in no way releases you from your responsibilities to harvest the Word. It's just the opposite. The Holy Ghost enforces the Word. I have often said that getting filled with the Spirit is dangerous, because that Consuming Fire burns off more than your bondages; He also puts a flame under you.[12]

Right in the midst of your visitation and blessing, Jesus begins His work as "refiner and purifier," turning up the heat on you to the end that you will "offer unto the LORD an offering in righteousness."[13]

You can either cooperate with the Baptizer by lining up with the Word, or you can fight His efforts of discipline. Whichever choice you make, all impurities *will* surface and God *will* deal with them. The outcome of perfection or ruin is up to you.

Led to the Word

If you were to drive on the highway to my hometown in Pennsylvania, you would encounter a sign along the road, maybe sixty miles or so away, that says: "Williamsport." Now, what if you were to stop at that sign? Could you say that you were in Williamsport? No. Though you have, indeed, reached a visible expression of Williamsport, the sign is only pointing you to an ultimate destination. Signs point beyond themselves.

Never mistake spiritual gifts as being the ultimate goal of the Christian experience. The Holy Ghost is giving these gifts as signs that point beyond their own manifestation. This is where many of my fellow Spirit-filled brothers and sisters have missed it. A lot of them seem to live for big events, sensational meetings, and their next spiritual experience to outdo their last. All they care about are grand finales. I am here to tell you that regardless of how powerfully He manifests, the Spirit never comes as your escape from the world; He comes as your triumph in the world by revealing Jesus Christ.

Jeremiah prophesied of New Covenant believers that God would put His "law in their inward parts ... writ[ing] it in their hearts,"[14] and Ezekiel made it clear how that would happen:

> And I will give them one heart, and I will put a new spirit within you; and I will take the stony heart out of their flesh, and will give them an heart of flesh: that they may walk in my statutes, and keep mine ordinances, and do them: and they shall be my people, and I will be their God.
>
> — *Ezekiel 11:19-20*

The baptism of the Holy Ghost should never be seen as a side dish to Christianity, but neither should it be treated as something more advanced than the Word. Let me remind you that the Word is the *result* of the Spirit.

No prophecy of the scripture is of any private interpretation. For the prophecy came not in old time by the will of man: but holy men of God spake *as they were* moved by the Holy Ghost.
— *2 Peter 1:20b-21*

All scripture *is* given by inspiration of God.
— *2 Timothy 3:16a*

To those pastors who say you are Spirit-filled, please listen to me. Getting the Word into your church members means more than whipping them through a few weeks' worth of generic Bible classes. Such sloppy work shows a lack of genuine burden for the flock of God and falls short of your full duty. To do it God's way, sow and re-sow the Word. New believers must learn it, older saints should review it, and all have to live it. Besides, it is only by cultivating the Word that there is *guarantee* for future manifestations of the Holy Ghost, hence the "fruit of the Spirit," and hence the warning, "Grieve not the Holy Spirit of God."[15] If you want to stay Spirit-filled, be filled with what the Spirit inspired—the Word.

Greater Power

I mentioned my brother Mark earlier. A few years ago, he and I visited with an evangelist who had extensively traveled in South America and who had witnessed some of the mighty revivals there that have swept tens of thousands of people into the Kingdom. As we talked, the subject of spiritual warfare came up and we asked the preacher, "Why is it that in South America, spiritual warfare seems to be so successful while here in the States we see it as being nothing more than a fad?"

116

Without hesitation the brother replied, "Well, from what I have seen in Latin America, pastors have general prayer teams, people that are praying all the time. But when it comes to something serious, like when witchcraft is involved, they have an elite prayer team made up of people who are living a holy life. These are the *only* people who the pastors will assign to do spiritual warfare."

That was an eye-opener! Not because his explanation was anything new to us but because in a day when holiness is either condemned as being old-fashioned or demoted as an internal-only quality, we found yet another confirmation that obeying the Word is directly connected to moving in the Spirit.

The gifts are important and valuable, and they are the will of God, but without practicing good, biblical behavior you will not be as mighty in the Spirit as you could be. Unless you use the gifts to point to the Word and fortify the gifts with the practice of the Word, your operation in them will lack richness, depth, and lasting affect in the lives of those whom you touch. The gifts confirm the fruit, but then the fruit fuels the gifts. Each witness of Christ complements the other.

Too few Christians realize there is as much power in the fruit of the Spirit as in the gifts. Forgiveness trumps hate. Righteousness destroys immorality. Self-control gains the advantage over chaos. I could go on and on, but when you begin to see into the spirit realm, you understand it is the godly virtue of the Word that finally uproots the powers of darkness. To keep a proper perspective, bear in mind that at the Second Coming the gifts will come to an end;[16] Jesus' words, on the other hand, will never pass away![17]

117

Oh, that believers would know the full authority of Jesus Christ![18]

> And they went forth, and preached every where, the Lord working with *them*, and <u>confirming the word</u> with signs following. Amen.
>
> *— Mark 16:20*

For a most powerful demonstration of the Spirit, for a maximum intensity of the Anointing, do the perfect thing and keep believing, keep living, and keep preaching the Word. Braid your enthusiasm and your operation in the gifts with the strands of Scripture and you will see the book of Acts come to life. It is like the saying we had in Bible school:

> Just the Word and you will dry up;
> Just the Spirit and you will blow up;
> But with the Word and the Spirit, you will grow up.

CHAPTER EIGHT REVIEW

1. Jesus is both the Sower of the Word and the Baptizer of the Holy Ghost, therefore have both the Word and the Spirit.

2. The Gospel is meant to make something happen, to bring tangible experience as well as inner belief.

3. Even while others are using gifts for their own good, God still wants to do supernatural things through His children. "Some may abuse it, but I'm gonna use it."

4. When you forget the Seed, you will grow the weeds.

5. When God pours out His Spirit on you, He is pointing to and confirming Jesus, not you.

6. When God manifests gifts through you, it is ultimately for the benefit of others and the Kingdom, not for self-promotion.

7. In the midst of your visitation and blessing, the Lord will turn up the heat on you. You will either fight Him or cooperate with Him.

8. The Holy Ghost gives gifts that point beyond their own manifestation. Additionally, the Spirit does not manifest as your escape from the world, He comes as your triumph in the world by revealing Jesus Christ.

9. Without fortifying the gifts with biblical behavior, you will not be as mighty in the Spirit as you could be.

NINE

Heavenly Minded, Earthly Good

By introducing God's battery key, I do not imply that we will eventually have all the answers to life's complexities. There will always be tension in our tiny minds over the how's and why's of divine dealings—that is the way it is! Nevertheless, by using the battery key, we inferiors can acquire the ability to discern the seasons and times, know how we must behave, and in that way be perfect before the Lord.

Ever hear that saying, "He's so heavenly minded, he's no earthly good?" There is a lot of truth to that. I have known believers who are so focused on escaping this world to the sweet-by-and-by that they pathetically neglect present responsibilities. Their home is a mess, their relationships are a nightmare, their unsaved boss is hopping mad at their laziness—but, oh, how ready they are for Glory. Or so they say! Such imbalance has injured their lives and brought shame upon the Church of God. On the other hand, there are supposed saints who cannot be distinguish from shameless sinners. Polluted with a life-enhancement gospel and bloated with self-esteem, these are so *earthly* minded they are no *heavenly* good.

What is needed for these two extremes? God's battery. We are the salt of the earth, but we are also "strangers and pilgrims" desiring "a better country, that is, an heavenly."[1] Yes, the meek shall inherit the earth, but there is also a crown, a reward, a treasure laid up for us in Heaven.[2]

Let me sum it up this way: It is the Lord's will that you have a vision of Heaven and at the same time be useful on Earth.

Heavenly Minded

Speaking of vision, why should you look for a city yet to come, "whose builder and maker is God?"[3] Because there are times when practicing faith in Jesus will make no sense to your feelings, your carnal mind, or the customs of unbelievers. There are times when choosing the righteousness of Christ will cost you promotions, relationships, and privileges, losses from which you may never recover. There may also be times when you sow and water seeds of the Word, maybe on the mission field or in the life of an individual, yet never see the fruit of your labor. That's OK. There is more on life's color palette than earth tones.

Because Jesus is the light of the world and because it is the Spirit of God who influences man in that light, understand that you must have your eyes on Christ if you expect to be focused and make right choices. Without the guidance of the Lord in your life, you will default to your deficient human outlook. You will follow the selfish, succumb to the shallow, and be in constant danger of deception and sin, for without a vision for Heaven you can only look forward to Hell.

To keep the right perspective of all that God asks of you and succeed in perfection, you must, as Paul said:

> Set your affection on things above, not on things on the earth.
>
> — *Colossians 3:2*

While you must look beyond yourself, you must also look beyond the opinions, sentiments, and behavior of man. Others of flesh and blood can easily touch your heart and win you over. If you allow them, their human influence can hold a strong, manipulative power over you. In convincing you they have your best interests in mind, people have the ability to make the wrong seem sensible, the better choice. They can make your opinions appear so small and narrow compared to theirs. They can also put incredible pressure on you with threats as well as conditional promises.

Depending on others for acceptance and meaning is what the Bible calls "the fear of man," and it is a trap.[4] It is a preference that will damn your soul, for the Bible says:

> If I yet pleased men, I should not be the servant of Christ.
>
> — *Galatians 1:10b*

Never think that you are, all by yourself, impervious to human influence. You are human and you identify with what is human. Without a determined focus upward, you will, at some point, be swayed and make compromises of personal ideals, let alone excellent principles, just to win prizes from hands of clay.

We need to be lifted above earthly impressions to a greater view; we need the mind of Christ. When we think like Jesus and think with Jesus, we are able to behave with clarity, foresight, and complete understanding; and we find the integrity to stand for truth, regardless of people's threats or their applause.

Heavenly Rewards

Living for front-loaded satisfaction and how you can get ahead right here, right now leads to sacrificing what eventually means most. Of course, those without a godly view do not even care. Until the day their play-now-pay-later lifestyle catches up with them. Then, it is too late!

Another reason to be Heavenly minded is that those things which are truly important and which really perfect us rarely bear fruit overnight. Honor, integrity, and credibility are descriptions awarded to one's reputation only *after* consistency. Like the seeds that first root underground before sprouting on the surface, you have to be patient for godliness to take full effect.

For instance, people almost never jump in your path and say, "Hey! You are impacting me. Your faith and your words are convincing me of Jesus Christ and His goodness." It would be nice if they did. You could know that you were being useful. But people are just not like that. Often, it is only when something bad happens to them or to you that they realize what is in their heart. Therefore, despite what responses you are or are not getting from people, be conscious that your strong example for Christ speaks volumes to those around you. Whenever they respond (if *ever* they respond) makes no difference. You are going to keep shining that light and throwing out that Seed because you are shining and sowing for Jesus, not man.

> So then neither is he that planteth any thing, neither he that watereth; but God that giveth the increase.
>
> — *1 Corinthians 3:7*

To us who believe in the Truth, our ultimate reward is not on Earth anyway. Whether we find prosperity or persecution for our faith, we are running for a prize found *after* this life.

As Paul wrote to the Philippians, the reason we count both the success and suffering of this life as loss is because the only thing that matters is winning Christ. Our labor and motives are wholly different from a world rushing to manufacture their own brand of righteousness. Our goal is found in Jesus and His righteousness that we might "attain unto the resurrection of the dead."[5]

We believers know if a person sows to the flesh, if he trusts in and practices what seems good in this life, he will reap corruption and destruction in the Last Day. We also know that if someone sows to the Spirit, if he trusts in Jesus and practices His Words of Life, the Lord will raise him from the dead and he will reap immortality, "life everlasting."[6]

Properly Placed Glory

There is one more very important reason why we should look for "the things which are not seen."[7]

At one point during His earthly ministry, Jesus appointed seventy of His disciples to go to various cities and prepare the people for His arrival.[8] Apparently they ministered over the sick as well as publicized meetings because the disciples returned to the Lord "with joy," reporting that "even the devils are subject unto us through thy name." Jesus confirmed their enthusiasm and their supernatural gifts, but then He made a statement that, at first, seems strange, even anticlimactic.

> Notwithstanding in this rejoice not, that the spirits are subject unto you; but rather rejoice, because your names are written in heaven.
>
> — *Luke 10:20*

In saying this, Jesus was showing the seventy the correct way to receive God's benefits.

Yes, we need to have the right attitude toward God's benefits because it is possible to use them for personal gain and private indulgence. This is true for moving in spiritual gifts, as did the seventy, but this is also true for being the recipient of grace in general.

A present-day abuse of divine favor is exposed in the not-so-rare statement, "God sent Jesus because He could not live without us." This contemporary outlook on salvation is nothing more than a humanistic retooling that falsely exaggerates man's importance, declaring that we as individuals have preserving merit and *deserve* to be saved. This and all self-glorification is evil in the eyes of the Lord and one thing that God absolutely will not share with anyone—including His saints—is the position of exaltation.

I will not give my glory unto another.
— *Isaiah 48:11b*

God has no needs, He is obligated to no one, and He wants all the credit for our blessings. God knows He is God.

Whatever the Lord does to us, for us, and through us is *always* to be considered outstanding generosity; but unless you are heavenly minded, you will unavoidably neglect to give the proper gratitude and worship that is due the Lord. You will be blind to the hand of Providence in your life, mismanage merciful resources, and be in danger of the gross sin of pride, which God hates.[9]

Oh, there is a season and time for boasting, but even then, it is never for self-gain. When we are used of the Holy Ghost and when others recognize virtue or benefits in our lives, we must insist on showing our own inadequacies while ranting and raving about the greatness of our God.

But he that glorieth, let him glory in the Lord.
— *2 Corinthians 10:17*

Jesus was not discouraging the seventy from moving in the supernatural nor was He suppressing them from expressing joy and excitement. He was simply using the battery key and setting priorities straight. Glory is for Heavenly use, not Earthly profit.

Earthly Usefulness

Make no mistake, being heavenly-minded is not a mystical quality you privately possess. It's not about *feeling* spiritual. If you are truly heavenly-minded, you will be of *much* earthly good, for Earth is the platform on which heavenly things are performed.

A lot of people around the world think that being sold out to God's service means leaving normalcy and living a life of solitude, poverty, and celibacy with no other occupation but prayer and meditation. Though it sounds especially sacred, though there may be a scattered few who are thus called, this otherwise elitist, separatist idea is absolutely the wrong practice of heavenly mindedness.

Is this my opinion or does this statement have the weight of biblical righteousness in it? Just look:

> If thou sinnest, what doest thou against [God]? or *if* thy transgressions be multiplied, <u>what doest thou unto him</u>? If thou be righteous, <u>what givest thou him</u>? or what receiveth he of thine hand? Thy wickedness *may hurt* a <u>man</u> as thou *art;* and thy righteousness *may profit* <u>the son of man</u>.
>
> — *Job 35:6-8*

Wow! Did you get what you just read? Your naughtiness and rebellion can never destroy the Kingdom of God, never have, never will. However, your wickedness does "hurt" others. Likewise, your good deeds and godly character will never make you irreplaceable to the Self-sufficient One, but your holiness does profit others.

When you are living as a hermit, you may, with your bystander philosophies, seem a spiritual expert, but the real godly authorities are those living everyday life, walking through all its ups and downs and successfully exemplifying the Lord Jesus Christ. Again, this is more than my opinion. The New Testament is rich with verses showing that God views piety in much more down-to-earth, person-to-person ways than we may like:

> *This is* a faithful saying, and these things I will that thou affirm constantly, that they which have believed in God might be careful to maintain good works. These things are good and profitable unto men.
>
> *— Titus 3:8*

> And let us consider one another to provoke unto love and to good works.
>
> *— Hebrews 10:24*

> Let your light so shine before men, that they may see your good works, and glorify your Father which is in heaven.
>
> *— Matthew 5:16*

True holiness is supposed to change Earth, not impress Heaven. Families, friends, and associates need to profit from your wholesome and upright interaction. Neighborhoods, schools, and churches need the influence of your godly input. Politics, business, education, media, medicine, the whole scope of this lost and dying world needs to be able to look at your public conduct, find answers, and get hungry for God.

We twenty-first century believers should not think that the Gospel is an earthly welfare program that allows us to do as we please, but neither should we hide in shadows of seclusion awaiting a breakout from this life. This is our hour to master living by living for the Master. We must look to Heaven, work on Earth, and show the world how God's battery works.

CHAPTER NINE REVIEW

1. It is the Lord's will that you have a vision of Heaven and at the same time be useful on Earth.

2. Why be heavenly-minded? Unless you have your eyes on Christ Jesus, who is the light of the world, you will fail to make right choices. Without a vision for Heaven, you can only look forward to Hell.

3. We need the mind of Christ to gain the superior view of life and stay focused.

4. Things that are truly important and that really perfect us rarely bear fruit overnight, and you cannot always measure the effectiveness of godly things by their beginning.

5. To us believers, our ultimate reward is not found on Earth.

6. Why be heavenly minded? You will be blind to the hand of God in your life and thus neglect to give the proper gratitude and worship that is due the Lord.

7. Your sin cannot hurt God but it does hurt others; likewise, your good deeds do not profit God but they do profit others.

THE KINGDOM KEY

TEN

Time to Grow Up!

When someone first comes to the Lord, it is not unusual for his life to be riddled with problems. There are personality messes to clean up, situations that need to be put in order, and circumstances that need nothing less than divine intervention. Soon, the Lord begins working and miracles seem to explode everyday like popcorn. The young convert is glowing with testimonies of how he led this hard-nosed person to the Lord, how that family matter was marvelously healed, and the way in which God used a certain Scripture to bring a lifelong, inner turmoil to a sudden end. Right before his very eyes, the person's old life vanishes and the possibilities and promises of the Kingdom become brighter and brighter.

All of this excitement is very good and very normal, but something inevitable happens. The new believer soon becomes a *seasoned* believer. He becomes established in good behavior, disciplined action, and godly thinking. He grows familiar with biblical doctrine, he develops a habit of devotions, and he becomes faithful to a local church. He no longer surprises anyone when he carries his Bible to work, walks away from a dirty joke, or bows his head before his meals. Everyone expects it. He is a Christian.

This, too, is very good and very normal. Yet somehow, Christians see this now settled life as being a backslidden life. They look at all the awesome things they experienced as a young believer and they think that similar fast-paced events should still be happening. "When I was *really* on fire for God …" is what they say.

Well I am here to tell you that your routine and orderliness are not hard evidence of being lukewarm. For young Christians, the dynamic of newness causes *automatic* interest and enthusiasm; but newness in the Lord is meant to *wear off*, just as childishness is supposed to wear off.

Many times I have heard pastors say, "When we started this church years ago, we didn't know what we were doing. We were kids. But somehow the Lord led us and we can now look back at all the great things God did." At hearing this, I have often gotten the impression the pastors really meant to say their present ministry had become too mature, too aged, and it was their youthfulness, spontaneity, and ignorance that were responsible for glory-days accomplishments.

Well, dear pastor, when you were a young minister, success and growth came, indeed, but it came by *accident*. Guess what? This walk with Jesus is not about theme-park thrills or the ever-changing changes of adolescence. Newness was a stage in which you no longer live.

God still wants you to depend totally on Him, but as a seasoned saint He now wants your success, your growth, and your zeal to come by *experience* and *deliberate action.*

Everyone enjoys and needs the enthusiasm from a new believer. Everyone should be excited about a new church or a new pastor. God's process, however, eventually leads a person and a work beyond novelty to something more substantial and influential—maturity.

There is a movement in the Church today in which people who have been saved for a significant amount of time are talking about crawling up in God's lap, giving Him hugs and kisses, and playing as a little child before Him. Well I have an important announcement: God wants you to grow up! While having faith like a child is commendable, being childish is not. There are many things you can only be and do as a *grown* son or daughter in the faith. Kingdom authority, not eternal kindergarten, is the key Christ eventually hands you. Are you going to know how to use that key?

Growing Up in Love

Perhaps the most important area in which people of our time need to immediately grow up is a full understanding and practice of true love. Everyone is preaching about God's *agape,* His unmerited love signified by "affection and benevolence"[1] toward us, and everyone is teaching how we ought to show charity[2] to each other, and both of these things are invaluable truths, to be sure. Yet who is completing the picture by talking about how we ought to agape[3] God?

This may come as a shock, but according to the Jesus, loving God is *the most important* love priority:

> Thou shalt love the Lord thy God with all thy heart,
> and with all thy soul, and with all thy mind. <u>This is
> the first and great commandment</u>.
>
> —*Matthew 22:37b-38*

True, to love others is *proof* that we love God,[4] but to love God is a *yielding to* and *provision for* love in the first place. For God *is* love!

In our unregenerate state, we all too often love things that are depraved, foolish, and ruinous. If that were not bad enough, our basic approach to love is blaringly humanistic. So like our view of perfection, not only is our kind of love imperfect, it is polluted! Even in our dearest relationships we inescapably filter love with selfish motives and ungodly perceptions. In doing so what we exercise and experience turns out to be a deceptive paint job covering dysfunction. Sadly, the same goes for a lot of us church people. Because our love for God remains in lower-nature mode, we continually contradict and destroy the very perfectness for which we yearn.

Jesus taught that we need to seek *first* the Kingdom of God and His righteousness; we need to love God above everything else. He also taught that unless we hate father, mother, siblings, spouse, children, assets, and our own lives also, we cannot be His disciple.[5] In other words, if we love the things and people of this world first, we cannot possibly exercise right or perfect love or grow as justified sons and daughters of God who work divine righteousness in the Earth. Jesus' teaching exposed a truth we don't like to accept: We give in to either heavenly interests or earthly ones for it is impossible that both loves coexist as top priority.[6]

Understand that the kind of love the Bible lifts up before us is not your kind, not my kind, not the feelings-based kind, but Christ's kind. Make no mistake about it, Christ's love is predominantly focused on Father:[7] His heart, His will, His Word, and His Kingdom come first. Yes, Jesus' love is the requirement to perfect love, but again it is also the further production of perfect love; it forces us to grow up beyond the easy, baby stage of "me" and it refines and corrects our growing sense of "we."

Forget all the grandiose ideas out there. When it comes to making tough, significant decisions, as a person or as a people, the tipping factor is always love. We need only look at present secularism to see that man-centered affection corrupts into an irreverent, materialistic, counter productive culture; anemic of principles and conditioned for collapse. However, when we love God first, it follows that we will love truth, goodness, and justice. The charity that we have towards our fellow man becomes enriched and counterbalanced with pure intentions and righteous guidelines.

Let me ask you: Are your love priorities in or out of order? You ask the Lord for everything that interests you, but when is the last time you sought for the things that interest the Lord? When is the last time you prayed, "Not my will but thine be done," and then waited to move forward until God showed you the answer? Does it deeply concern you that, in an evil generation, both the King and the Kingdom retain a good reputation, and therefore you do or say *nothing* that would ever disgrace that reputation? Are you so thoroughly convinced of Jesus Christ and His Gospel that whether it is pain, heartbreak, persecution, loss, or times when it is difficult to understand what and why Father is doing, nothing can separate you from the love of God? Are you really growing up?

The Advantages of Maturity

At some time or other, you may have stopped to enjoy the majesty and beauty of a big, old oak tree, but did you know that an oak does not begin producing acorns until it is at least twenty years old? Sometimes it will take up to fifty years before the first yield. Only when it reaches seventy or eighty does it become really fruitful, dropping thousands of acorns and increasing production year after year. Even after it reaches 100 and slows down, it will still produce acorns by the thousands.

The Bible says:

> Better _is_ the end of a thing than the beginning thereof.
>
> — _Ecclesiastes 7:8a_

Look around. Babies do not shape the nation. Children do not control society. Even with the worldly cult of youth worship, not even teenagers run things. I know that for me, there are things I can do now as an adult that I could never do as a child, a teen, or even as someone in my twenties. There are qualities that I have now which were, at best, premature and misplaced when I was younger. Personally, I am glad for the years I have, and if there ever was such a thing as a time machine, I would have no desire to return to the days of stupid pranks, silly clothes, and awkward behavior.

While we should urge young people to "go forth and conquer," the real movers and shakers of this world are those who have built up influence, reputation, and resources. Power and fulfillment actually belong to the mature, the accomplished, or, in the biblical sense, the perfect.

It is the same in the Church. Glory, leadership, and stability, let alone society-changing revival, do not come from babes in Christ. Despite personal charisma or potential, those who are spiritually imperfect or immature are incapable of reproducing what they themselves lack. Recent history alone conclusively proves the Church suffers when the shallow and shoddy are at the helm; yet when the disciplined and determined are leading the charge, those who have a developed sense of Kingdom responsibility and grown-up love, success and strength, effectiveness and happiness come in their wake.

Those who have been prepared and experienced in the Lord, who have built up reserves of tested faith and proper perception, who have denied their flesh and defied their fears; only they have the godly range of leadership that can impart a thorough, workable vision to a generation needing light.

In your seasoning with God, you have, or will have, definite advantages that were unavailable to you before. Learn to tap into the benefits of your maturity, which comes as you grow in Christ. It is one thing to have spiritual power but quite another to administer that power with full effect. Just as Jesus "waxed strong in spirit"[8] increasing in "favour with God and man,"[9] learn to make the most of your solid and godly reputation, your skillful insight, and your understanding of God's ways.

Now the God of peace, that brought again from the dead our Lord Jesus, that great shepherd of the sheep, through the blood of the everlasting covenant, <u>make you perfect in every good work to do his will, working in you that which is wellpleasing in his sight, through Jesus Christ</u>; to whom *be* glory for ever and ever. Amen.

— Hebrews 13:20-21

No, you cannot afford to level off in your faith but neither can you afford to waste your Christian life chasing new experiences or living in shallow, self-serving emotions. There is a world to win, a Kingdom to inherit, and a King to love and serve. It is time that you grow up and be responsible or perfect in your calling. That is what the rest of this book is all about.

CHAPTER TEN REVIEW

1. When it comes to the things of the Lord, the dynamic of newness is meant to wear off, just as childishness is supposed to wear off.

2. Young believers often find success and growth by accident. As a seasoned saint, God wants that success and growth to come by experience and deliberate action.

3. While loving others is proof that we love God, loving God is a yielding to and provision for love in the first place. Loving God is both qualifier to and refinement of perfect faith.

4. Only those who have been prepared and experienced in the Lord have the range of leadership that can impart a thorough, workable vision to a generation needing light.

5. After you become established in Jesus Christ, you learn that it's not about you.

6. If you are of Christ Jesus, then you will do what He does and love the Church. You will become an asset in the assembly where the Lord places you.

7. The mature believer knows that one or two bad trees do not condemn the whole forest. If you are going to work with people, even church people, you are going to get hurt, but the destination is worth it.

8. A grown child of God will never cause other believers to stumble into sin, even if it costs them a liberty or a privilege.

9. If you really love God, the Church, and the sinner, your top priority will be to live an ideal example of Christianity, doing and saying nothing that would disgrace the reputation of the King or the Kingdom.

10. God does not need protection. However, the knowledge of God must be kept from being misrepresented.

11. Experienced believers should realize that besides sin and gray areas, there are bad habits that can destroy young believers. These habits must be avoided.

ELEVEN

An Addiction that Hinders Perfection

When I was in elementary school, I had a teacher who thought it would be good to introduce us city kids to growing a garden. She gave each of us a little container and showed us how to fill them with soil, bury three or four seeds, and then add some water. She instructed us to put our names on our containers and then find a place for them on the large sill that ran all the way across the windowed wall.

The teacher reminded us each day to water, and within a week or so all the containers had little shoots sprouting up. We were all excited. First thing in the morning, we ran to inspect our plants. One day, we found two fresh, bright green leaves had opened up, Another day we found tiny branches had developed. It seemed that every time we looked, our miniature gardens showed us something new.

After a while, our living project took over the windowsill and the teacher said it was time to take the plants home. She told us they were strong enough to grow outside and if we wished we could replant them in our backyard. What a pleased little boy I was, carrying my container home to show Dad and Mom something I could now do all by myself!

* * * * *

When a person is young in the Lord, it is normal and necessary that a spiritual leader looks over his shoulder and walks him through the details of the Christian life. It is also normal and necessary that a new believer learns to respect and be loyal to his godly oversight, submitting to them for their work in the Lord. Yet the day comes when that which *began under supervision* must be *transferred to personal responsibility* if it is going to continue to develop.

God intends on making you and me "kings and priests [who] shall reign upon the earth,"[1] people who are individually strong for Christ and who will stand in the Kingdom on our own two feet. The problem is, there are many who are still too fond of the sill.

Preacher Addiction

Over the years, I have had people approach me and say, "You gotta keep on me, Pastor. I need you to keep calling me so that I stay on the 'strait and narrow.' You gotta get me to church on Sundays." When they have spent a good amount of time on the windowsill and are still talking like this, I know these people have what I call *preacher addiction*.

In my experience, people of this mindset are secretly on the look out for loopholes. They are willing to do everything the preacher tells them, but they are also keen to do everything the preacher *does not* tell them. If they can get away with something without being officially rebuked, then they justify it. These are similar to the people who say, "If God didn't want me to do that, He could have made me stop." *They want to be forced to live right.* Pretending the responsibility for their soul belongs to someone else, they refuse to recognize for themselves how carnality and spiritual laziness keep them undeveloped. They hide behind their self-imposed ignorance saying, "As long as my church and my preacher don't have a problem with it, it's all right, right?"

> Surely these *are* poor; they are foolish: for they know not the way of the LORD, *nor* the judgment of their God.
>
> — *Jeremiah 5:4b*

I have found that when people are in chronic need of a ministerial babysitter, it is not because they are merely unstable or unhealthy in the Kingdom. Rather, it is a sign they are holding back from making a full-fledged commitment to the Lord Jesus Christ.

Preacher addiction can actually be more subtle than this, and there are way too many in the Body of Christ who, when they ought to be teachers, are still babes. They have been saved and in church for years, but they are still walking around waiting for someone to tell them what to do; waiting for the next book, the next television program, the next big seminar, the next high octane preacher to inspire them to go farther. They may not be looking for loopholes, but they have telltale signs of addiction:

- Having a faith that is numb (no evidence or substance in the soul), the individual lacks internal motivation and must constantly be pumped to perform spiritually.

- Conduct and practice are not based on conviction but in thoughtless performance of religious tradition and custom.

- They are unable to explain from Scripture why they believe what they believe.

- Nearly all their private devotions consist of listening to or reading someone else's devotions.

- To them, getting to know the Lord means looking to commentaries and theological works of others, instead of seeking God for themselves.

- Their spiritual moods hinge on what local and national ministries are doing or not doing.

- They look forward to the day revival falls so they can get on fire. Until then, ... well, that is what they do not want to own up to.

- They feel that only when their pastor gives a certain sermon can things change in their community, church, or home. They do not see themselves as being the ones liable for bringing real impact.

Whether by unawareness or laziness, *anytime* a believer depends too much on church leaders there is preacher addiction.

Hero Worship

The critical danger of preacher addiction is that even experienced churchgoers can quickly crossover into the lethal land of hero worship. There, appreciation for a leader mutates into unconditional allegiance and robotic obedience. This is more common than you may think.

Disappointing as it may be, there is no virtue in believing something just because a celebrated personality said it is so. Furthermore, it is faulty to assume that you are in the right simply because you are loyal to what your family, your denomination, or your favorite minister believes. If your convictions do not match up with God's Word, your faith and your faithfulness are in vain.

Flesh is flesh. Regardless of how unique, how moving, how significant, how famous, how sincere, how right, or how anointed they are, flesh is flesh. If you get your eyes off the King and His Kingdom and get caught up in all the fascinating distinctions of an individual and his ministry, you will be filled with flesh and will only produce flesh.

I know people who point to and quote their favorite preacher more than they do Jesus—and with more reverence. I know people who have backslid because the national ministry they so stanchly adored fell. I also know people who, with eyes wide open, marched behind their religious favorite into sin and heresy, because "They were right then, they must be right now." But none of this is true loyalty or devotion. This is going too far. This is hero worship.

It is time we the saints stop turning ministers into celebrities. A preacher can become selfish and magnify himself, but an audience can magnify a preacher too. Yes, honoring those who labor in the Word is right and good,[2] but we often become unreasonably enamored with certain men and women of God, awestruck by their gifts and accomplishments. We elevate their personal histories as patterns guaranteed to bring certain results and we gobble up their teachings with no questions asked. Imitating others can only go so far. Following preachers as if they were little messiahs destroys them as an individual, destroys their ministries, and destroys the effectiveness of the Kingdom.

We must get our eyes off of what great people do and look at what great people see. Truly distinguished saints set their sights on the glory of God in Christ. Jesus is their secret to success. He is the focus that gives them their rock-solid assurance, the inspiration that produces their miracles, and the voice that leads them to their outstanding victories. It is Jesus who we are really seeing, living in and through the mighty—and outliving them as well.

Healthy Reliance

The whole reason we become devoted to certain spiritual leaders is because every one of us has a real and personal void that must be filled. We need a bigger-than-life legend that will provide a higher purpose to our existence. We need a superstar who will champion the Christian cause, a great one we can rally around, and an authority on whose conclusions we can build. I am here to tell you that there is such a One. He has come as God in the flesh and is the Greatest of the great, the Lord Jesus Christ. He is the Preacher to whom we must be addicted, the Hero who we must worship.

The true Church has never pivoted itself on pulpit ministry. Preachers can point you in the right direction, but they are not meant to be the Church's jack-of-all-trades nor are they called to be supervisors over some spiritual daycare. Those who watch for our souls and labor in the Word are called for the purpose of rooting us in Jesus Christ so that we may all function as one Body in Him.

> And he gave some, apostles; and some, prophets; and some, evangelists; and some, pastors and teachers; for the perfecting of the saints, for the work of the ministry, for the edifying of the body of Christ: till we all come in the unity of the faith ...that we *henceforth* be no more children, tossed to and fro ... but speaking the truth in love, may grow up into him in all things, which is the head, *even* Christ:
>
> — *Ephesians 4:11-15*

Sooner or later you have to take your own container off the windowsill and make personal contact with the Lord all by yourself. You have to "give diligence to make your calling and election sure."[3] Yes, you will come to the same conclusions as millions before you—the Spirit will always confirm the Word— but it will be *your* revelation, grafted in by Christ. God is looking for self-starters, people who are individually strong in the faith, strong enough to stand alone, strong enough to be planted anywhere.

Standards of Success

If people have to withdraw from preacher addiction, preachers have to withdraw from instigating that addiction. Ministers need to learn from a brother in the Lord who, in using his Kingdom key, stayed true to Christ's perfection: the apostle Paul.

While preaching in Lystra with Barnabas, Paul commanded a crippled man to stand up.[4] Immediately the man was healed by the power of God and stood to his feet. Because of that, an epidemic of preacher addiction broke out. The people immediately prepared sacrifices to the two preachers, cheering, "The gods are come down to us in the likeness of men!" Unlike some today who would welcome such an event, Paul tore his clothes (an ancient custom showing distress, displeasure, or grief), and ran among the people with Barnabas crying, "We also are men of like passions with you!" It was all he could that day to put out the flame of false fame.

In no way did the apostle see this kind of excitement as advantageous. Paul was not in Lystra to promote his personal ministry; he was there to preach the name of Jesus and repentance from sin. He had a Kingdom mindset, and he refused to accept man's applause and praise as his compensation. Paul refused to *feed* their addiction or to *feed off* their addiction.

* * * * *

If in the last few decades there has been a wave of ministerial idolatry, it is must be admitted that many believers have adopted standards of success of what a preacher or a church should be, standards that have little to no Kingdom significance. Having a megachurch does not mean you are more spiritual than a pastor with a few dozen members; it may simply mean you live in a highly populated area. Being on TV does not prove you are better than other ministries; it may only indicate you know how to raise money or you have personal connections with station owners. There are plenty in the ministry who have grabbed the spotlight, not by the call or provision of God, but through hobnobbing, marketing techniques, and other foul-smelling, self-promotion strategies. Let's get honest!

Now we all know that having thousands in your church is not wrong, and neither is ministering in front of cameras or being well-known. There are ministers in the forefront of attention who are there by the calling of the Lord. They have something legitimate and vital to say, and we need such figures of integrity and grit. What is wrong, however, is to use carnal currency to estimate a minister's Kingdom value, to set up a hierarchy based on fame, status, and the size of one's audience. That is sin!

Never assume that having a lot of resources at your disposal (money, workers, connections) or that headline notoriety are automatic signs of God's blessings on your life, let alone signs of success in the ministry. You can be a big name yet be as ungodly as a sinner with as little love for the people of God. I know because I have met ministries like this.

Besides, when the Lord puts a man or a woman in the public eye, who but the proud would insist that person has "made it" and should fight to stay there? It may be, and often is, that God calls individuals to the forefront with a timely word and for a particular season; but then moves them on to some private post where they will continue to be most useful. Only those without Kingdom priorities would define such people as has-been's when God calls them obedient.

The bottom line is: whatever you use as a standard of success will become your bending point. If large audiences are your measurement, then you will, for example, sacrifice true conversion for feel-good, non-offensive altar calls, just to "keep 'em packed in." If having your book or CD in the number one slot is your measurement, then you will sacrifice spiritual meat for church-flavored junk food just to get sales. If, however, being faithful to the call of God is your gauge, if "present[ing] every man perfect in Christ Jesus"[5] is your measure, then you will sacrifice your reputation, your privacy, your possessions, and even your so-called golden opportunities of high-profile ministry, just to see souls come to the Truth.

A Prophetic Word

Titles, fame, money, approval from the world, none of these things in and of themselves are useful to the Lord. What God wants to know is, "Where are those who want My Kingdom to be promoted?" Unless those who are now in the spotlight start exercising Kingdom priorities, God will replace them with those who will. In fact as I write this, I feel the Spirit of the Lord upon me, saying:

> "This superstar mentality that has plagued the Western Church has got to go! There is coming a shaking!

> "There are those reading this book who have relied too much on what you have learned and what you think you have become. You have relied too much

on the alphabet that is on your wall. You have relied too much on your title. You have relied too much on the arm of the flesh and you've not gone in on your knees; you haven't been praying and seeking God. You are dry. You are dead; and if you'll get honest, you haven't had a good time in the presence of God for a great many years.

"But I have news for you, even you who are the 'upper crust.' You're dead and you're dry but if you will humble yourself and seek my face, says the Lord, I will raise you up and I will do things for you that you could only dream of doing. Because truly, this is the time of winnowing my harvest. I am going through the grain and separating the wheat from the chaff; and many who looked like wheat will be discovered as chaff, but many who were looked down on as chaff shall be wheat. And they shall harvest and bring forth wheat, says the Lord."

Multi More Than Mega

False standards in the ministry are just another product of the ladder model, where perfection is measured by "how high you climb" and "reaching the top." Church people actually use those terms. Using the ladder, however, has opened the door to the devil, who in turn has infected believers with condescending attitudes and dog-eat-dog competition, qualities that are dead wrong in the Body of Christ.

To encourage growth to the Body, and to discourage wrongful addiction, we all need to use the Kingdom key and see the

Kingdom picture. There is no room for ministerial elitists, strutting their stuff and looking down their noses at all the "little" ministries as if they were somehow defective and pointless. Ministers must have a utilitarian mindset and realize that every true Christian work is crucial to spreading the Gospel. The Body needs people who are going to think as a unit and teach the rest of us to do the same, so that Jesus Christ may be seen of all men.

Yes, there ought to be churches in New York and Paris, London and Hong Kong, but I think of the churches that are in the real majority. The little ones. I think of the churches that dot the countryside or stand on Main Street in some remote and tiny town. I think of the congregations that meet in school buildings, basements, store fronts, hotel conference rooms, empty sections of a factory, or, as I have seen in Kenya, out in the open under shady banyan trees. I think of the groups that are singing with accompaniment music because they do not have any musicians, of those who have to share a pastor with nearby villages, and of all the wonderful Sunday casserole dinners that will never make the news but will serve as love feasts, bringing fellowship and unity. With all their provincial oddities and predictably obvious defects, all of these individual groups are God's heart and part of the greater Body; and as promoter of the Kingdom, all of these deserve your appreciation.

Those who can stir the souls of thousands are important, but no more so than that one on the street corner leading a stranger to Christ. In hospitals, jails, factories, libraries, schools, and on ships that sail the Seven Seas, as well as in government, finance, education and business, recreation. We need to raise our voice for Jesus Christ everywhere.

The real success of the Kingdom is gauged not so much by *mega* as it is by *multi*, a genuine Christian influence felt everywhere!

Ministers must grow in appreciation for each other's God-designated function and realize that no matter the scope of one's responsibility, there are always pluses and minuses. Sure, the big ministries can make contact with more people, but with big ministry comes big problems. OK, small ministries may have improper equipment and lack modern facilities. Maybe the way they do things is sometimes awkward and even corny, but they love on people unlike anyone else in the world, and they fill needs unlike any organization could ever dream.

This is God's army, Heaven's Kingdom, and it is unimaginably massive. Nobody but Christ Himself could organize or maneuver such a varied, fast-moving congregation. In areas both crowded and remote, Jesus constantly sends His laborers. He causes a few of them to be known far and wide, but most need no such recognition. Christ has made them scattered treasures for His glory, hidden throughout the world and prized by all who find them.

The Gospel is making much progress in the earth, but you have to have the Kingdom key to be part of it.

Do you want to know who the real losers in the Kingdom are? You may be shocked. Some have huge assemblies, worldwide programs, audiences with international leaders, and popularity that rivals an entertainment star. Those who fail to make the grade are the ones using non-Kingdom standards of success, the ones who "seek their own, not the things which are Jesus Christ's."[6] They don't realize the real competition for the Church is true versus false, not big versus small.

Not a Ruling Class

In the pure sense, the ministry is a function fundamentally *opposed* to the idea of spiritual haves ruling spiritual have not's. Ordering lowly laity around and ministering down to people— feeding an addiction—is wicked, unchristian practice. The goal of church leadership is "that we might present every man perfect in Christ Jesus."[7] That can never be realized as long as people cling to the feet of gilded ministers.

Something extremely important to get in your spirit: *the ministry is not a promotion.* It is nothing you earn. Ministry is a job, an assignment, a responsibility, and in no way does it put you in an upper class with perks and privileges only a clerical order deserves.

Yes, the ones who are in your care are to honor you because of your labor in the Word. Yes, they are to receive you as one sent in the name of the Lord. Yes, they are to follow you as you follow Christ. Yet when all is said and done, you are a fellow citizen in this Kingdom with every other believer. You are a saint, but those to whom you minister are saints too. You are just as prone to weakness and loss of direction as anyone else. Furthermore, you are obligated to the same standards, guidelines, and principles as anyone else—but all this humanness is exactly what God uses.

People do not need leaders who are above their struggles and questions, angels in glistening white. People need "men with like passions," those who know how to follow Christ to ripeness and completion through daily winding pathways, those who can impart a hearty, red-blooded faith.

A new day is dawning in the Body, a day of growing up for all the saints of the Most High—ministers included. You might have to change your view of who you are. God has called you to be a facilitator, a coach, a hands-on guide who considers others as being more important than yourself. You are a fellow traveler pointing the way and saying, "Here is what the Lord wants from you and by the grace of God, you can do it!"

And that leads us into the important message of the next chapter.

CHAPTER ELEVEN REVIEW

1. When a person is young in the Lord, it is normal and necessary that a spiritual leader looks over his shoulder. Yet the day must come when that which began under supervision must be transferred to personal responsibility if it is going to continue to develop.

2. People in chronic need of a ministerial babysitter are not just unstable and unhealthy, they are holding back from making a full commitment to the Lord.

3. Anytime a believer depends too much on man there is preacher addiction.

4. Get your eyes off the King and His Kingdom, get caught up with an individual and his ministry, and you will be filled with flesh and will only produce flesh.

5. Preachers can point you in the right direction, but they are not meant to be the Church's jack-of-all-trades nor are they called to be supervisors over some spiritual daycare.

6. It is a sin to estimate a minister's value based on fame, status, and the size of one's audience.

7. It is time to use the Kingdom key. We need ministers who realize that every true Christian work is crucial. We need ministers who think as a unit and will teach the Body to do the same.

8. The real success of the Kingdom is gauged not so much by *mega* as it is by *multi*.

9. The ministry is not a promotion. It is a calling, a job, a responsibility, and in no way does it indicate an upper class.

TWELVE

Ministering for Perfection

E verything you go through as a believer (and specifically as a minister) is to be used for the furtherance of the Gospel. Those personal victories and blessings, they are not for your trophy collection. You have been given them to glorify the Lord and infuse others with faith. Even your trials and mistakes can in some way be utilized for the advancement of the Kingdom. *Your very being*, in fact, is tool and medium for the Master's use. You, the person, become God's real-time opportunity for touching human souls. Therefore, if you are to affect any real, perfect Kingdom gain, you have got to walk the talk, live the Christian life in spirit and in truth.

Jesus said of ministers:

> A good tree cannot bring forth evil fruit, neither *can* a corrupt tree bring forth good fruit. Every tree that bringeth not forth good fruit is hewn down, and cast into the fire. <u>Wherefore by their fruits ye shall know them</u>.
>
> — *Matthew 7:18-20*

Here is the shock to a twenty-first century clogged with ministers desperate to be celebrities: Just as resources and popularity do not prove a minister's success; *gifts, talents, and accomplishments alone are not verifications of a minister's legitimacy.* The factor that distinguishes true from false, real from fake ministers is the produce, the harvest of that person's lifestyle. A minister is to be assessed in this way[1] because their real self is the quality that makes the biggest impression.

The proverbial do-as-I-say-not-as-I-do technique is as undesirable in ministry as it is anywhere else and yet for one added reason: the dimension of the unseen.

Allow me a negative example: Years ago, a certain pastor who I knew very well began traveling regularly to a particular country for mission trips. At first, he did the smart thing and took others with him. Soon after he insisted that he travel alone, and that was that. Before long, a strange phenomenon began in his church: long-time, solid members—leaders included—began to have major marriage problems, and some entered into adultery and divorced their spouses. The church started falling part!

People soon found out the pastor had secretly been having his own affair with a woman on the mission field. His hidden sin openly influenced everyone under his care. True, the individuals had a choice; yet it was the pastor, the human channel, who had introduced and encouraged adultery into his congregation, not by words or even by show, but simply by what he himself had become.

Allow me another example: As part of a team, I was invited to a church who wanted to introduce proper prophetic ministry into their area, and I remember a kind of polarization existing in those particular meetings. The people in that church were very open to the prophetic, but at the same time the team found it difficult to operate in prophecy. We thought perhaps it was the enemy opposing the power of God; so we just plowed through and the Lord, in fact, spoke to His people.

At the last meeting, an old prophet showed up, not to minister but just to sit in on the service and fellowship with the other attending preachers. After the meeting was over, it worked out that I was to drive this man of God and another brother back to the hotel where we were staying. Insisting on sitting in the back seat, the old prophet said nothing for the first half of the ride, but at one point he blurted out, "It's too bad none of your prophecies are going to stick!"

The car went silent.

Then I asked, "What do you mean?"

The old prophet shot back, "The reason you had such a hard time was because that is not a praying pastor and that is not a praying church. None of those prophecies are going to take root because they are not a praying people."

I knew from what I saw in the natural and in the Spirit that the veteran preacher was right; and to this day, I can still hear his words sounding in my soul like a bell: "That is not a praying pastor!"

Ministry: it's not who and what you know, it's who and what you are.

* * * * *

Paul understood Jesus' words about the kind of fruit a minister produces, which is why he wrote to the believers in Rome:

For I long to see you, that I may <u>impart</u> unto you
some spiritual gift, to the end ye may be
established;

— Romans 1:11

Impart means "to give over" or "share."[2] Paul knew what he
had to give over or share was more than information; it was
something spiritual, something that had to be passed on in
person.

Peter understood Jesus' words also. Look at what he said to
the lame man at the Gate Beautiful:

Silver and gold have I none; but <u>such as I have</u> give
I thee: In the name of Jesus Christ of Nazareth rise
up and walk.

— Acts 3:6

We all know God healed the lame man that day, and yet the
Holy Ghost was flowing out of *Peter's* belly,[3] out of Peter's
"such as I have."

The question I want to ask you is: what is your "such as I
have?" What are you imparting?

Preacher, ministry is much more than what you do behind the
pulpit or during working hours. God has sent the people *you.*
Ministry is you, publically and privately.

Forget the theories about ministry, you have to accept the
facts of experience: education, formality, and performance will
never produce life by themselves. Like cheap remodeling that
only covers but does not fix, these inanimate items are hardly

the stuff of ministry. Never put ultimate confidence in such things. Rather, concentrate on the condition of your being. Your spirit, your mannerisms, your personality—*you* are the conduit! Ministry is by *your* fruit! If you are carnal, you will have carnal people. If you are weak, you will have weak people. If, however, you are filled with faith, if you are fervent in prayer, if you follow after holiness, if you hunger for and joy in the Lord, then those following you will pick up on and reflect the same things.

As my old Bible School teacher used to say, "Some things are better caught than taught."

Working to Perfect the Body

Whether you are a full-time pastor, a part-time chaplain, or an active volunteer in a home Bible study, you need to ask yourself, "Why am I in the ministry?" For some people, they have a grievance to air, an opinion to promote, piety to show off, or a desire to be the new circus in town. Still others are ministers simply to pull a paycheck, to preserve a dead denomination, or because someone such as Mom or Pastor Pete expected it of them. None of these are worthy motives! Being a real man or woman of God is about laying your life down and becoming the "filth of the world," the "offscouring of all things"[4] so that others may be strong and rich in Jesus Christ.

> Now ye are full, now ye are rich, <u>ye have reigned as kings without us</u>: and <u>I would to God ye did reign</u>, that we also might reign with you.
>
> — *1 Corinthians 4:8*

167

On one hand, there is "the anointing which ye have received of him abideth in you, and ye need not that any man teach you."[5] Non-ministry saints should, indeed, be looking to Christ, not a preacher, for their completion. Yet on the other (and here we use the battery again), unless you as a minister have it in your spirit to bring the Body to perfection, experience proves that those under your care will hardly, if ever, find maturity in Christ. You cannot give something you do not have, and you cannot expect people to learn and practice what you are not.

We know God answers prayer and gives us the desires of our hearts. So what happens when, as a minister, your prayers and your desires are toward the Kingdom? What happens when your prize, the thing you are deeply hoping and fighting for, is to see others come to maturity and produce full results? The earth sees a strong Church, rich in faith, abundant in power, and growing by leaps and bounds.

The world is tired of weak, apologetic people in the pulpits and we of the twenty-first century have had our fill of the plastic, Hollywood-type ministers who have nothing better to do than beg for money. It is time for true ministers to rise to the forefront, those who love the truth and who love the Body more than anything in the world! It is time the Church had strong examples of morality and integrity, and it is time for the Earth to shake from men and women who are radiating with the Holy Ghost. We do not need those who are profiting from church; we need those who are working to perfect it.

If you are in the ministry for something other than the Kingdom's sake, do the Church and the world a favor, my friend, step aside.

Jesus' Building Method

Having begun treading the unpopular path of truth, I may as well go all the way: You, as a minister, are a representative and servant of God, *not* of the people. Only when you become thus minded will you find the strength to give the Church what they *need*, not just what they *want*. As well as encouraging saints in the positive side of the faith, you regularly will have to address people's philosophies, habits, and even cultural assumptions for the sake of leading them to perfection in Christ Jesus. If you are a me-centered ministry, the negative side of the battery will seem counter productive; but if you love the King and His Kingdom, you will refuse to look the other way. You will confront! Besides, if your flock is to stand for truth, you must show them how.

Scores of pastors and even whole denominations center their entire ministry on the rebel and the sinner, trying to get them to come in, feel good, and be fond of Christians. From the color of the carpet to how long a sermon should be, many churches have become impotent and wishy-washy because they are trying to make the Kingdom fit man instead of man fit the Kingdom.

Preacher, while you focus all your time and energy on making unconverted goats happy, the sheep—"over the which the Holy Ghost hath made you overseers"[6]—are starving! Your tap-and-dance services may be drawing a crowd but they bring no valuable change and do nothing for the Body. Jesus, on the other hand, has a much better method for building the Church. He came for the entire world, but do you know the group He focused on and poured into the most? It was His disciples, those who committed to the truth and submitted to Him.

Let me put it this way, if all your sermons are efforts to motivate the stubborn, lukewarm, and lazy, you will always be on the defense—and there is no gaining in that mode! If, however, your sermons, prayers, praise, and activities center around what God is saying and doing to and through His Church, saints get fed and grow strong. Subsequently the whole congregation becomes a bustling hive producing the honey of righteousness, peace, and joy. Something else happens. Sheep (as someone has pointed out) beget sheep. When a flock is well-rooted, their speech, their works, and their authority in a perverse generation draws new converts and turns countries and cultures upside down.

The ironic thing is, when people come under a ministry with a Kingdom theme rather than bless-me motives, they actually gain a greater sense satisfaction and Christian identity than otherwise; and the minister, in turn, will have more to give and be more effective.

How about it, preacher? Are you ministering for perfection?

CHAPTER TWELVE REVIEW

1. Gifts, talents, and accomplishments alone are not verifications of a minister's legitimacy. According to Jesus, a minister is assessed by their "fruits" because this is what actually influences others.

2. Ministry is you, publically and privately.

3. Unless you as a minister have it in your spirit to bring the Body to perfection, those under your care will hardly, if ever, find maturity in Christ. If the Body is to have Kingdom thinking, then Kingdom thinking must be in you.

4. Pastors and even whole denominations try to make the Kingdom fit man instead of man fitting into the Kingdom.

5. Ironically, when people come under a ministry with Kingdom motives, they will actually receive more from the minister and, in turn, the minister will be more effective.

THIRTEEN

Time to Peddle

I remember the time a neighborhood friend taught me to ride a bicycle. I had asked him if he would show me how and he said he would. I don't remember everything he told me (it's been over 30 years), but I remember he remained on his bike and talked and talked and talked. He showed me what this was and how that worked, what one should and should not do, and I seem to remember that he told me a bunch of his riding experiences. Even after I finally mounted the rickety contraption, he kept right on talking, reminding me of all the things he had said. Know what? Despite all the information I had received, it was not until he let go and I started peddling that I learned how to ride.

The teacher in me says there is more, so much more to perfection, and yet it is an unfinished ending that I believe will do you the most good. I have showed you what God showed me: how perfection is really a garden, a battery, and a Kingdom key; and even more basic, it is a living, everyday relationship with a Savior who personally knows human nature. So at this point, you do not need me to go on gabbing, you simply need to start peddling.

If there is just one other thing I ought to say before the bike starts rolling, it is this: Everything I have presented to you in Jesus' name has been about God's ways and God's thoughts. Never forget that you, the earthy creature—with all your collection of opinions, emotions, experiences, and homebrewed religion—are your own greatest hindrance to satisfactory development and mature performance. To reach your God-intended ripeness, you must learn to trust explicitly in the One who can keep you from falling, for it is faith in the Lord Jesus Christ—His power, His Word, His image—that is the ultimate key to perfection.

So stop worrying. And stop over analyzing everything, too. Simply let go of your own brand of perfection and take off with the kind that is wonderfully attainable.

Endnotes

Chapter 1: Are Christians Supposed to be Perfect?

1. Exodus 20:3
2. These and similar definitions of "perfect" are easily found by doing a word study in the *Strong's* Hebrew and Greek dictionaries.
3. Public Domain
4. Ibid.
5. Copyright © 1993, 1994, 1995, 1996, 2000, 2001, 2002, by Eugene H. Peterson
6. Copyright © 1996, 1998, by International Bible Society
7. Copyright © 1996, 2004, by Tyndale Charitable Trust. Used by permission of Tyndale House Publishers.
8. Copyright © 1995, by American Bible Society
9. Ephesians 3:19
10. Genesis 6:9; Job 1:1; Luke 1:5-6
11. Colossians 4:12; Ephesians 4:15-16; Romans 14:19
12. Romans 12:2; 2 Corinthians 13:9; Ephesians 4:11-15; Hebrews 13:20-21; 1 Peter 5:10; 2 Peter 3:14
13. Hebrews 2:10
14. Ephesians 4:11-12
15. 2 Samuel 22:33
16. John 1:9
17. Hebrews 12:2 The word "finisher" here means "completion, perfection." See *Strong's Greek Dictionary*, 5047.
18. In Haggai 2:7, Christ is called the Desire of All Nations.

Chapter 2: Forbidden Perfection

1. Mark 7:13

Chapter 3: God's Perfection

1. Isaiah 61:1-3
2. Colossians 2:6-7
3. Galatians 6:7
4. Ibid. 5:22-25; Romans 7:4
5. John 15:2-6
6. Genesis 17:1
7. Luke 8:11
8. Matthew 7:24
9. 1 John 2:3-4
10. John 15:14
11. Matthew 7:21; John 5:24, 38-40
12. John 15:5
13. Ecclesiastes 12:13
14. Micah 6:8
15. 2 Peter 1:5-7
16. Matthew 22:37-39
17. Luke 18:8
18. James 2:19; Mark 1:24; Acts 16:16-17
19. Judges 13-16
20. Acts 9:5
21. 1 John 5:3
22. Psalms 119:35, 47
23. Philippians 4:4
24. Nehemiah 8:10

Chapter 4: Dealing with Mistakes Perfectly

1. 2 Corinthians 4:7
2. John 1:14; Philippians 2:6-8; 1 Timothy 3:16

3. John 3:19-21
4. Ibid. 8:1-11
5. Leviticus 20:10
6. Revelation 2:22
7. Ibid., 1:29
8. 1 John 3:8
9. Ibid. 3:5; John 14:30
10. Romans 12:9
11. Jude 1:23
12. 1 Timothy 4:2
13. Hebrews 4:16 The Greek word for "grace" is *charis* and it means acceptable, benefit, favour, gift, grace (-ious), joy liberality, pleasure, thank (-s, -worthy). See *Strong's Greek Dictionary*, 5485.

Chapter 5: The Hardest Thing to Handle

1. Galatians 3:3
2. Romans 1:21-32
3. Matthew 12:45
4. 1 Corinthians 9:27
5. Philippians 3:18-19
6. Job 5:7
7. Genesis 1:26-28
8. Psalms 75:7
9. Deuteronomy 8:18
10. Proverbs 8:12

Chapter 6: Two Sides to Perfection

1. Proverbs 6:16
2. 1 Samuel 2:6

3. Isaiah 9:6
4. Exodus 15:3
5. Colossians 3:11; 1 Corinthians 15:28; Ephesians 1:23
6. Ephesians 2:9
7. Philippians 2:12
8. Ecclesiastes 3:1
9. Ibid. 8:5
10. Matthew 5:48
11. Ibid. 5:44
12. 1 Corinthians 1:30
13. Ibid., 1:12-13; 3:4
14. Revelation 3:19a

Chapter 7: Of Fear and Love

1. Matthew 10:28; Romans 11:20-21; 2 Corinthians 7:1; Ephesians 5:21; Philippians 2:12-13; Hebrews 4:1; 12:28; 1 Peter 1:17; 2:17; 3:15; Revelation 14:6-7
2. 1 Corinthians 16:22; Galatians 1:8-9; 2 Peter 2:12-15
3. Acts 12:21-23; 13:9-11; Revelation 8-9; 22:18
4. James 1:6-7; 4:3; 1 Peter 3:7, 12; *with* Acts 10:35; 1 John 3:22
5. Revelation 14:7
6. 1 John 3:18-22; Romans 2:12-16; Titus 3:10-11
7. John 16:7-11 In this passage, the word "judgment" (*krisis* in the Greek) literally means "decision."
8. 1 Peter 3:12
9. Luke 6:46; Matthew 7:21-23
10. Matthew 5:16; John 14:23; Hebrews 5:9; Revelation 2:5
11. John 6:29 See also John 3:36; Psalms 2:12; Mark 16:16; Romans 10:3

12. This would include the works of the Oral Law, which Jesus vehemently denounced as being opposed to true obedience. In the books of Romans and Galatians, Paul makes it clear that the works of the Law are not true faith. It is important to realize this distinction from the other "good works" in the New Testament.
13. Ephesians 2:10
14. 1 John 4:20
15. 1 John 5:2 "By this we know that we love the children of God, when we love God, and keep his commandments."

Chapter 8: The Word and The Spirit

1. Ephesians 4:13
2. Matthew 13:37 with Luke 8:11
3. Matthew 3:11
4. Mark 5:25-30
5. See *Thayer's Greek Dictionary*, under the Strong's correlating number, 1411.
6. I hate making the distinction between Bible and Spirit camps, but I believe it is the best way to explain my point. It is, in fact, a distinction that exists in people's minds, though it should not.
7. Acts 17:6
8. 1 Thessalonians 1:5
9. Ephesians 3:20
10. 1 Corinthians 14:40
11. Numbers 22:22-31
12. God manifests His grace not just to give you another chance, but more so to make you another person. Colossians 3:9-10; 2 Corinthians 5:17
13. Malachi 3:1-3
14. Jeremiah 31:33

15. Ephesians 4:30
16. 1 Corinthians 13:8-10
17. Matthew 24:35
18. Proverbs 28:1; John 14:30

Chapter 9: Heavenly Minded, Earthly Good

1. Hebrews 11:13-16
2. 1 Peter 1:3; 5:4; 2 Timothy 4:8; Matthew 19:21
3. Hebrews 11:10
4. Proverbs 29:25; 1 Samuel 15:24
5. Philippians 3:8-11
6. Galatians 6:8
7. 2 Corinthians 4:18
8. Luke 10:1-20
9. Proverbs 8:13; 6:16

Chapter 10: Time to Grow Up!

1. See *Strong's Greek Concordance*, #26.
2. Another word translated from *agape*.
3. Examples of *agape* and *agapeo* toward God: Matthew 6:24, Romans 8:28, 1 Corinthians 8:3, 1 John 5:2-3
4. 1 John 4:20
5. Luke 14:26, 33; Matthew 10:37
6. Matthew 6:24 "No man can serve two masters: for either he will hate the one, and love the other; or else he will hold to the one, and despise the other. Ye cannot serve God and mammon."
7. John 8:29, Psalms 40:7-8, Revelation 1:5
8. Luke 2:40
9. Ibid., 2:52

Chapter 11: An Addiction That Hinders Perfection

1. Revelation 5:10; 1:6; 1 Peter 2:5-9
2. 1 Timothy 5:17; Philippians 2:29; Hebrews 13:17; 1 Corinthians 16:15
3. 2 Peter 10
4. Acts 14:8-18
5. Colossians 1:28
6. Philippians 2:21
7. Colossians 1:28

Chapter 12: Ministering for Perfection

1. 1 Timothy 3:1-12; Titus 1:5-9; Acts 6:3
2. *Strong's Greek Dictionary*, see #3330
3. John 7:38-39
4. 1 Corinthians 4:13
5. 1 John 2:27a
6. Acts 20:28
7. Ibid. 6:10

Michael Holcomb is available for speaking engagements and personal appearances. For more information contact:

Michael Holcomb
BibleDays Ministries
PO Box 2515
Williamsport, PA 17703

www.bibledays.org

contact@bibledays.org

To purchase additional copies of this book or other books published by Advantage Books call our toll free order number at:
1-888-383-3110 (Book Orders Only)

or visit our bookstore website at:
www.advbookstore.com

Longwood, FL. USA
we bring dreams to life
www.advbookstore.com

LaVergne, TN USA
16 February 2010
173274LV00004B/3/P